Population
and
Society

Studies in Sociology

CONSULTING EDITOR:

CHARLES H. PAGE

University of Massachusetts

Population and Society

DENNIS H. WRONG

New York University

Third Edition

RANDOM HOUSE · NEW YORK

THIRD EDITION

9 8 7 6

© COPYRIGHT, 1956, 1961, 1967, BY RANDOM HOUSE, INC.
All rights reserved under International and Pan-American
Copyright Conventions. Published in New York by Random
House, Inc. and simultaneously in Toronto, Canada, by Random House of Canada Limited.

LIBRARY OF CONGRESS CATALOG CARD NUMBER: 67–22323

MANUFACTURED IN THE UNITED STATES OF AMERICA
by The Colonial Press Inc., Clinton, Mass.

TO TERENCE

Preface

So MUCH empirical research is going on today in the social sciences that many textbook writers tend to confine themselves simply to summarizing the findings of numerous research studies. The temptation to do this is particularly strong in the field of population study where decennial censuses and continuous records of vital statistics regularly supply demographers with vast mines of data to be analyzed and interpreted. Consequently, general conclusions are often subordinated to detailed enumeration of the evidence on which they rest, and the forest is not seen for the trees.

In this short introduction to the study of population I have tried to avoid overloading the text with statistical data and citations of research studies and have limited myself to stating broad conclusions supported by many different strands of empirical evidence.

The field of population study has, in recent decades, expanded to embrace so many diverse topics that coverage of all its main subdivisions is impossible in a study as short as the present one. In general, I have tried to increase the appeal of the book to sociologists concerned with the study of population by emphasizing population history, theory, the social and psychological determinants of fertility and migration, the nature of the "population explosion" in underdeveloped countries and the problems and controversies aroused by this explosion. The most serious omissions, given the impossibility of covering the entire field of population in so short a volume, seem to me to be the very scanty treatment of the consequences as opposed to the causes of population trends, the failure to consider systematically materials on population composition, and the failure to deal with urbanization as a demographic process.

I have incorporated into the section in Chapter 7 on "The Contemporary Population Debate" most of an article on the population explosion which first appeared in the *Providence Evening Bulletin* of March 3, 1960 and was later reprinted in a slightly longer version in *The New Leader,* September 5, 1960. Chapters 2 and 7 include paragraphs from my article "Population Myths" which was published in *Commentary,* November 1964.

I am grateful to Professor Edward G. Stockwell, now at the University of Connecticut, for making the computations on which Figure 2 is based. Professor Charles H. Page's editorial advice has been invaluable in improving the style and organization of the study and I owe him a considerable debt of thanks.

DENNIS H. WRONG

Contents

Population
and
Society

The Field of Population Study

Demography and Population Study

Why are people thickly clustered on one part of the earth's surface while far larger areas remain thinly settled? Why is one human community growing by leaps and bounds while another, which formerly grew just as rapidly, reveals a decline or stabilization of numbers? Why are families large in one society and childbirths frequent, while the opposite condition prevails elsewhere? Why does the frequency of births and deaths vary in successive decades or historical periods within the same society?

These are some of the questions that students of population attempt to answer. Today the study of human populations is often known as *demography* and its practitioners as *demographers*. Yet only a part, though an indispensable part, of the entire field of population study deserves this name. The demographer *qua* demographer is likely to concern himself with a narrower range of questions than those raised above. He wants to know what the actual size of a population is, its rate of growth or decline, and whether the change reflects changes in the numbers of births, deaths, or migrants or some combination of these. He is concerned with measuring, usually by complex and technical methods, the quantitative changes a population exhibits before he goes on to ask questions about the whys and wherefores of the trends he discovers. It may appear from this account that the demographer confines himself to apparently simple, descriptive or "factual" questions while the full-fledged population analyst (often in fact the same person) pushes beyond these to deal with the more fundamental and interesting level of causal explanation. But the demographer's task is by no means simple and, as Kingsley Davis observes, he is often justifiably suspicious of the sociological or economic theorist of population because of "the latter's inability to get straight the facts of population that he is presumably explaining." [1]

The data and skills of the demographer, therefore, lie at the core of the field of population study, although the field also deals with issues transcending them. Since demography is so central to the field, any effort to indicate the scope of population study must begin with a definition of demography.

Demography may be most broadly defined as the statistical description and analysis of human populations. More specifically, it is a discipline that aims at ascertaining the numbers and distribution of people in a given area, the changes in their numbers and distribution over time, the age and sex composition and the birth and death rates of a population, and the mathematical interrelations among these various quantities. Some definitions of demography also include measurement of the territorial movements of people, or migration, and the statistical description of characteristics of the population other than age and sex, such as marital status, occupation, religion, or race.[2] Demography is necessarily a quantitative discipline for its data are quantities to begin with; numbers constitute its very object of investigation. Changes in the size of a population result from changes in the numbers of births, deaths, and migrants, so these three variables, sometimes known as the "components" of population change, are, in addition to population size itself, the fundamental quantities which the demographer handles. Since births and deaths are taking place continually, and since people frequently change their places of residence, the demographer is interested in these common experiences as on-going processes which he calls *fertility, mortality,* and *migration.* These are the three basic demographic processes.

When the demographer seeks to discover the causes and consequences—social, economic, and political—of population trends, he necessarily leaves the realm of pure statistical measurement and draws upon those physical and social sciences which study the different kinds of events that impinge upon the basic demographic processes. There are students of population, chiefly those employed by government census bureaus or in actuarial work for life insurance companies, whose work is largely confined to formal demographic measurement, but most specialists in the study of population on the staffs of universities and private research agencies are unlikely to draw a very sharp distinction between those aspects of their work that are purely demographic and those aspects bearing on the "causes and consequences" of demographic trends. Yet the distinction between "demography" and "population studies" is useful for analytical purposes.[3]

Population Study and the Social Sciences

Population study is unavoidably an interdisciplinary field. As Hauser and Duncan assert, it is not and cannot be "a single 'theoretical discipline' with a coherent frame of reference of its own."[4] Population change is a concrete phenomenon to the understanding of which sociologists, economists, biologists, and other specialists contribute. In Kingsley Davis' words, "fertility, mortality, and migration are all to a great extent socially determined and socially determining. They are the inner or formal variables in the demographic system, whereas the outer or ultimate variables are sociological and biological. Whenever the demographer pushes his inquiry to the point of asking why the demographic processes behave as they do, he enters the social field." [5]

The medical pathologist helps the population student account for trends in morbidity and in the causes of death. The biologist explores the physiology of procreation and casts light on numerous factors affecting fertility. The geneticist clarifies the meaning for the hereditary quality of a population of differences in the rates of increase of various population groups. The economist helps the population student grasp the relationship between material resources, the state of the industrial arts, and the numbers of people an area can support. Sociological studies of the institutions of marriage and the family and of the religious and moral values associated with the universal human experiences of birth, illness, and death greatly illuminate the basic demographic processes. The work of geographers, political scientists, historians, psychologists, and psychiatrists also may have considerable bearing on the understanding of population phenomena. Valuable contributions to the field of population study have been made by pure mathematicians and statisticians on the one hand and, on the other, by speculative philosophers of history who have seen population movements as crucial factors in the rise and fall of civilizations. And all these various specialists may make use of the data assembled by demographers in working on problems in their own fields.

The natural sciences, as we have indicated, contribute significantly to the study of population. But the main causes of population trends, and the consequences of them that arouse greatest interest, are *social*. Human society is the man-made environment within which the demographic processes take place. Beliefs and attitudes towards sex and procreation, marriage customs and the structure of the family, economic and, increasingly today, political and military considerations play a large part in determining the frequency with which people have children. Levels of living, public health practices, and methods of treating the ill are closely related to the incidence of mortality. Ethnic and religious conflicts, territorial differences in economic opportunity, immigration laws, and the uprooting of peoples by war and conquest are the principal determinants of migration.

Because social factors are so central in the causation of population trends, the study of population is generally considered a branch of the social sciences. In the United States most scholars who identify themselves as demographers or as population specialists are sociologists by educational background, and population study increasingly tends to be viewed and organized for educational purposes as a sociological specialty.[6] In other countries, however, and at earlier periods in the United States, economics, geography, and the biological and medical sciences have been the major sources of population specialists. Most of the founders of demography and of population theory were economists and statisticians.

Whatever the academic classification of population study may have become for purposes of teaching and professional organization, the various areas of specialization within population study are unequally related to existing sciences and academic disciplines and their subdivisions. For example, the study of fertility is linked to sociological work on family structure and sex mores, whereas the study of mortality necessitates ties with the medical and biological sciences. As an acquaintance of the writer's, a sociologist seeking a sociologically relevant perspective on mortality statistics, once remarked: "The trouble with death is that it's so damned unmotivated!" Migration, on the other hand, is a topic that relates closely to many of the concerns of the economist as well as to such fields of sociology as human ecology and urban sociology. The problems arising out of the relation between numbers of people and resources, often referred to since the time of Malthus as "*the* population problem," are highly relevant to the economist's expertise and to his current interest in economic growth. In short, as Kingsley Davis remarks, "there is no such thing as a complete populationist, any more than there is such a thing as a complete sociologist or a complete economist." [7]

Population Characteristics

The population student is interested not only in the absolute numbers of people inhabiting a selected area, but also in their *characteristics*. He learns, for example, how the population is divided into groups or statistical categories differing with respect to measurable attributes such as age, sex, marital status, citizenship, rural-urban residence, occupation, and income. *Age* and *sex* are the most important population characteristics from the formal demographic standpoint, because they are directly related to fertility and mortality. Only women within a certain age span are capable of producing children, and people die more frequently at some ages than at others. The numbers of births and deaths, therefore, clearly depend to some degree on the age-sex composition of the population. *Marital status* is also an important population characteristic, for the institution of marriage is universal and in nearly all societies the vast majority of births are produced by married women. Marriage, in fact, is sometimes regarded as a basic demographic process of the same order as fertility, mortality, and migration, since trends in the number of marriages and the marital composition of the population are so closely related to trends in the number of births.

The other characteristics of the population studied by population students are selected mainly for two reasons: first, because of their strictly demographic significance, since most of them are related in some way to fertility, mortality, and migration; and second, because they are of intrinsic sociological or economic importance. Occupational groups, for example, usually differ with respect to fertility and mortality, and information about the occupational distribution of a population also indicates a great deal about its socioeconomic structure, aside from the possible relevance of such information to population trends.

Sources of Population Data

The primary sources of population data are national censuses and vital statistics. Demography is relatively new as a full-fledged field of special study because only in modern times have many nations begun making regular population counts which are reasonably accurate and complete. Even today reliable censuses have not yet been made in some of the backward or underdeveloped areas of the world and we must rely on estimates which are subject to wide margins of error.

A census is a periodic head-count of the population and some of its characteristics that is undertaken by the government. Clearly, only governments whose authority is generally recognized can effectively take a census. The lack of a strong central government in China is one of the main reasons why until 1953-1954 no census was ever taken of the population of that country. Moreover, only in countries with relatively advanced economies is the knowledge provided by a census sufficiently useful to justify its expense. Thus, with the exception of some colonial and semicolonial areas, censuses are regularly taken only in the advanced industrial nations of the world, and only since these nations underwent their industrial revolutions has census-taking become a generally accepted governmental activity. The first nationwide census of Sweden was taken in 1749, of the United States in 1790, of Great Britain and France in 1801, and of Russia in 1897, but most of these early censuses are unreliable in many respects and provide only scanty information about some major population characteristics.

The size and age-sex composition of a population as shown by a census give a static cross-sectional picture of the consequences at a particular time of past fertility, mortality, and migration. To study population growth dynamically, the numbers of births, deaths, and migrants must be known, requiring the continuous recording of vital statistics. We can, it is true, infer a great deal about past fertility, mortality, and migration from the "frozen" age-sex composition of the population that is glimpsed at the date of a census. But because census-taking is a costly and laborious affair which few nations can afford more often than once every ten years at the most, vital statistics are essential for the purpose of keeping track of population growth between censuses. By adding births and immigrants to and subtracting deaths and emigrants from the population enumerated at the last census, computation of the size of the population in intercensal years is possible.

In order to compare the "force" of fertility and mortality in different areas or at different times, the demographer requires a relative rather than an absolute measure of births and deaths, so "he relates births to the population in various ways to get birth *rates,* and he does the same with deaths and with migrants." [8] Vital statistics, consequently, are second in importance to censuses as a source of demographic data. However, accurate registration of vital statistics is even less common than the regular taking of censuses. Most modern countries began to take regular censuses long before they managed to achieve a fairly complete coverage of all births and deaths occurring within their borders. Not until 1933, for example, did the area within which births and deaths were accurately registered include the whole of the United States. Compulsory registration of births and deaths dates from 1874 in England and

Wales. Even in the highly industrialized countries, the registration of births and deaths is often less than 95 per cent complete in some areas, and in nonindustrial countries the recorded statistics should be viewed with considerable caution. As for migration, very few countries keep accurate records of immigrants and emigrants, the amount of migration usually being inferred from the increase (or decrease) in population over and above that resulting from the difference between the numbers of births and deaths.

In spite of unavoidable inaccuracies, modern demographers have developed ways of checking the reliability of census and vital statistics data. In contrast to the speculations of early writers on population, the general discussions of population trends in the remainder of this study rest on a firm empirical foundation.

World Population Growth and Distribution

Population Growth in the Premodern Era

Only in recent times has it been possible to determine with any accuracy the size, distribution, and growth of world population, and there are still large areas for which we must rely on fairly crude estimates. For the past the picture is even more uncertain. A few scholars have labored prodigiously in the field of historical demography to arrive at estimates of past population size and growth. And for the very remote past we are able to make rough inferences about the size and distribution of population from archeological knowledge of ancient civilizations and even earlier precivilized societies.

When men relied solely on hunting and food gathering for subsistence, the density of population and the total numbers of human beings on the earth were necessarily low. One of the most tangible effects of technological progress was an increase in the size and density of population made possible by a more abundant food supply subject to greater human control and permitting larger and more permanent settlements. V. Gordon Childe has identified three major technological revolutions which mankind has undergone.[1] The first, the *food-producing* revolution, took place initially about 8000 to 7000 B.C.; its main achievements were the invention of agriculture and the domestication of animals. The second technological leap, to which Childe gives the name *urban* revolution, apparently occurred for the first time about 4000 B.C. in the Nile valley and Lower Mesopotamia. It marked the birth of what we ordinarily call "civilization" in contrast to the mode of life of "primitive" or "preliterate" peoples, and resulted from a series of inventions and technical improvements making possible the appearance of cities as distinctive human settlements.[2] The third great revolution is, of course, the *industrial* revolution of modern times, whose impact on population growth constitutes so large a part of the field of population study today.

Childe and other historians of prehistoric and early historic times have attempted to determine when and where these revolutions first took place, but clearly they are processes of technological change that have occurred independently in various parts of the world at different times. Food-gathering societies still exist in remote corners of the earth today. The so-called contemporary "population explosion" is largely the result of the spread of the industrial revolution to areas that remain at the urban and, notably in parts of Africa, even at the pre-agricultural technological level. Each of the great technical revolutions transforms not only the economy but also man's entire way of life, and each produces a similar demographic effect: "an upward kink in the population curve."[3] Thus the world, or at least large parts of it, has witnessed "population explosions" before. It lends perspective to recall this, even though the rapid growth rates currently attending the process of modernization may have unprecedented aspects. We cannot be sure just how unprecedented they are when we lack the basic demographic data to measure the extent and timing of past explosions.

The great civilizations of the past fluctuated considerably in numbers and population density. Once they had completed an initial phase of expansion, however, the fluctuations probably evened out and numbers remained stable over long periods of time. Shifts of the areas of greatest density from the old centers of civilization to frontier regions probably occurred in all the continents that were the sites of major civilizations. Migratory invasions by "barbarian" peoples undoubtedly played a part in altering the distribution of population within the territorial limits of a civilization's cultural and political hegemony.

Population Growth and Distribution Since 1650

Two scholars, Walter F. Willcox and A. M. Carr-Saunders, have made estimates of world population growth and distribution by continent from 1650 to 1900.[4] Their series of estimates, which do not differ widely from one another, have been generally accepted as the most authoritative available. Carr-Saunders' estimates of the total world population run slightly higher than those of Willcox, but this difference is largely owing to rival estimates of the population of China, which has long been the unknown quantity of greatest magnitude in the world demographic picture. A recent exhaustive survey of the available evidence on Chinese population history tends to support Carr-Saunders' somewhat higher figures.[5] Table 1 shows Carr-Saunders' estimates from 1650 to 1900 as well as estimates made by the United Nations for several dates in the present century. The lower panel of the table shows the percentages each continent contributed to the world total from 1650 to the present time.

Although Asia still accounts for over half of the world's population and with Africa and Latin America is likely to show highest growth rates in the immediate future, Europe and the Americas have grown more rapidly since 1650. The Asian proportion of the world total has dropped slightly since the seventeenth century. In 1650 the Americas were inhabited by a small and scattered aboriginal population and the huge rela-

Table 1 *Estimated Population of the World and of the Continents, 1650–1965*

Continent	Population in Millions							
	1650	1750	1800	1850	1900	1930	1950	1965
Africa	100	95	90	95	120	154	198	310
Asia (excluding U.S.S.R.)	327	475	597	741	915	1,080	1,320	1,825
Latin America	12	11	19	33	63	109	162	243
North America	1	1	6	26	81	135	168	214
Europe and Asiatic U.S.S.R.	103	144	192	274	423	531	593	675
Oceania	2	2	2	2	6	10	13	17.5
World Total	545	728	906	1,171	1,608	2,019	2,454	3,285

Continent	Percentage Distribution							
	1650	1750	1800	1850	1900	1930	1950	1965
Africa	18.3	13.1	9.9	8.1	7.4	7.6	8.1	9.4
Asia (excluding U.S.S.R.)	60.2	65.2	65.7	63.1	57.8	53.5	53.8	55.5
Latin America	2.2	1.5	2.1	2.8	3.9	5.4	6.6	7.3
North America	.2	.1	.7	2.3	5.1	6.7	6.8	6.5
Europe and Asiatic U.S.S.R.	18.7	19.8	21.4	23.5	25.4	26.3	24.2	20.8
Oceania	.4	.3	.2	.2	.4	.5	.5	.5
World Total	100	100	100	100	100	100	100	100

SOURCE: United Nations, *The Determinants and Consequences of Population Trends,* New York: United Nations, 1953, p. 11; the figures for 1930 and 1950 are from United Nations, Population Division, "The Past and Future Growth of the World and Its Continents," in Joseph J. Spengler and Otis Dudley Duncan (eds.), *Demographic Analysis: Selected Readings,* Glencoe, Ill.: The Free Press, 1956, p. 28. The figures for 1965 are from United Nations, *Demographic Yearbook, 1965,* p. 103.

tive increases they show are the result of the settling of their almost empty territories by immigrants, largely from Europe. They have since maintained their rapid growth through high rates of natural increase, that is, large surpluses of births over deaths. Europe's population has increased more rapidly than Asia's because of a more favorable births-deaths ratio in the former during most of the period from 1650 to the present, although it has lost ground in recent decades.

The percentage of the world population accounted for by the continent of Africa has declined since 1650, but it is expected to increase in the next century. The decline is chiefly owing to the more rapid growth of other continents. Carr-Saunders believed that Africa's numbers declined absolutely between 1650 and 1800 as Table 1 indicates, whereas Willcox assumed no change in numbers over this period.[6] Recent writers have supported the latter, maintaining that Carr-Saunders overestimated the continental impact of the slave trade.[7] Central and South America may have experienced some decline between 1650 and 1750 when their native societies were destroyed by the Spanish conquerors.[8]

The bare figures showing the estimated size and distribution of the world's peoples reflect explosive and far-reaching historical events. These include the rise in the distant past of the ancient civilizations of Asia, which even by 1650 contained an estimated number of persons nearly twice that of the United States today; the tremendous release of human energies brought about by the industrial revolution in Europe; the devastations wrought by European invaders among the relatively primitive aboriginal populations of Africa and South America; and the great migrations overseas from Europe in the nineteenth and early twentieth centuries. All these events have contributed to the figures in the last column of Table 1.

Contemporary Population Growth Types

Although migration may play an important role for short periods of time, population growth depends largely on the numbers of births and deaths. The absolute level of birth and death rates is less important than the ratio between them. A population with a very high birth rate and a somewhat lower death rate will obviously grow more rapidly than a population with a birth and death rate that are almost equal, even if the latter's death rate should be considerably lower than the former's. There are four broad possible combinations of births and deaths: high birth rates may coexist with high death rates, high birth rates with low death rates, low birth rates with low death rates, and low birth rates with high death rates.

The last combination is clearly a lethal one. Historically, it has been found only in technologically backward societies subjected to ruthless military and economic exploitation by more advanced societies and, more recently, in those territories where expansionist totalitarian states have practiced genocide, the mass killing of civilian populations. Since only a small proportion of the world's peoples has met this fate, the fourth combination of birth and death rates is of less interest to population students than the other three.

Demographers have for some time been accustomed to classify existing populations into three broad growth types corresponding to the three main combinations of birth and death rates.[9] In recent decades, however, the growth rates of the world's nations and regions have varied so widely that a somewhat finer classification has been regarded as necessary. The Population Division of the United Nations has utilized a fivefold classification, defining the five types according to the following characteristics:[10] 1) high birth rates and high death rates, 2) high birth rates and declining but still fairly high death rates, 3) high birth rates and fairly low death rates, 4) declining birth rates and fairly low death rates, and 5) low or fluctuating birth rates and low death rates.

The only area exhibiting the Type 1 pattern of high birth and death rates is Central Africa. The data for this region are not very reliable, but it has long been the part of the world that is most backward technically and most isolated from the impact of modernization so it is probable that a stable pattern of high birth and death rates resembling that typical of "primitive" societies still prevails there.

Type 2, high birth rates and high but declining death rates, is represented by northern Africa and most of Asia with the exception of Japan. Considerable doubt exists concerning the growth rate of China.

Type 3, high birth rates and fairly low death rates resulting in a population that is growing more rapidly than anywhere else in the world, characterizes most of Latin America and southern Africa. The regions of Latin America that conform to this pattern are mainland Central America, the islands of the Caribbean, and the tropical countries of the middle and northern parts of the continent.

Temperate South America (Chile, Argentina, Brazil, and Uruguay), the Balkan peninsula, and the Soviet Union conform to the Type 4 pattern of declining birth rates and fairly low death rates. Their rates of growth have slackened considerably in recent years.

Type 5, the "modern" pattern of fluctuating birth rates and stable low death rates, is found in the most technically advanced countries of the world: all of Europe except the Balkan peninsula and the Soviet Union, North America except Mexico, Japan, Australia and New Zealand.

Some writers have argued in favor of splitting Type 5 into two separate types on the basis of growth trends in the years since World War II, to distinguish the older, more densely populated nations of Europe from such overseas countries settled by Europeans as the United States and the older British Commonwealth nations. Both groups of countries experienced a sharp rise in fertility during and after World War II, but European birth rates declined and stabilized at a somewhat lower level in the 1950's than birth rates in the United States, Canada, Australia, New Zealand, and white South

Africa. Immigration also continued to make some contribution to population growth in the latter countries. They exhibit, therefore, rates of growth that are higher than many Type 2 countries and almost as high as some Type 3 countries in spite of their moderate levels of fertility. Yet there is considerable justification for grouping them with the more stable European populations on the grounds that the acute sensitivity of their birth rates to social and economic conditions makes it possible for populations of this type to check their growth and even reverse it fairly rapidly.

Table 2 shows the present population, area, density, and growth type of a number of the world's largest, most populous, and politically important nations. The highest densities, it will be observed, are to be found in the older European countries, long the centers of Western civilization, and in the huge land masses of China[11] and India, the sites of ancient civilizations which have yet to undergo technical modernization but which, unlike most Type 1 and Type 3 areas, are already densely settled. The more recently modernized countries, with the important exception of Japan, are less densely settled and conform to Type 4 in their growth pattern.

The Theory of Demographic Transition

It is tempting to view the five growth types not merely as descriptive of the different growth patterns shown by the world's regions today but as stages of demographic evolution undergone by populations as they experience technological modernization. Such a conception is the core of what has come to be called transition theory. The notion of a demographic evolution correlated with stages in the process of industrialization has become the dominant organizing idea or theory in the field of population study since the discred-

Table 2 *Estimated 1964 Population, Area, Density, and Population Growth Type for Twenty Selected Countries*

Country	Population (in thousands)	Area (in square kilometers)	Density (1964 population per square kilometer)	Growth Type
Argentina	22,022	2,776,656	8	4
Australia	11,136	7,686,810	1	5
Brazil	78,809	8,511,965	9	4
Canada	19,271	9,976,177	2	5
China	690,000	9,561,000	72	2
Cuba	7,434	114,524	65	3
Egypt	28,900	1,000,000	29[a]	2
France	48,411	547,026	88	5
Germany				
Federal Republic	56,097	247,973	226	5
East Germany	16,028	107,896	149	5
India	471,624	3,046,232	155	2
Indonesia	102,200	1,491,564	69	2
Italy	51,090	301,255	170	5
Japan	96,906	369,661	262	4
Mexico	39,643	1,972,546	20	3
Nigeria	56,400	923,768	61	1
Pakistan	100,762	946,716	106	2
U.S.S.R.	227,687	22,402,200	10	4
United Kingdom	54,213	244,030	222	5
United States	192,120	9,363,353	21	5
Yugoslavia	19,279	255,804	75	4

[a] Cultivated area—34,815 sq. km.; Density—712.
SOURCE: United Nations, *Demographic Yearbook,* 1965.

iting of earlier efforts, of which Malthus' was the best known, to formulate universal laws of population growth and change.

Transition theory assumes that premodern populations maintain stability of numbers by balancing high, though fluctuating, death rates with high birth rates. As they begin to experience the effects of modernization, improvements in nutritional and health standards reduce mortality while fertility remains high and rapid growth ensues. Later, urbanization and other social changes associated with the more "mature" stages of industrialism create pressures favoring smaller families, and the birth rate falls, once again approaching balance with the death rate but at low (though fluctuating) rather than high levels. Only the fully modernized societies of western Europe, North America, and Australasia have, according to the theory, reached this final stage; most of Africa is still at the initial stage of high mortality and fertility. The other regions of the world display growth patterns reflecting different degrees of progression from the initial to the terminal stage according to their level and rate of economic development. This conception of world population growth in recent times is widely regarded as a genuine theory because it suggests predictions about the future growth patterns of the world's underdeveloped areas and therefore amounts to more than sheer description of past and present trends.[12] Figure 1 illustrates the theory diagrammatically.

Transition theory has been subjected to mounting criticism in recent years.[13] To begin with, it is thought to represent a crude, conceptually primitive model of population change that fails adequately to separate causal from descriptive propositions. As Robert Gutman has observed, transition theory continues "to have the character of an empirical generalization, since the rationale presumably implicit in it has never been systematically stated." [14] Essentially, transition theory generalizes from the historical pattern of population growth followed by western Europe in the past three centuries, holding that contemporary underdeveloped areas will recapitulate this pattern as they experience economic progress. Yet even if the demographic transition is considered simply a descriptive model, recently accumulated evidence from a variety of sources casts doubt on its empirical accuracy with reference to both the European past and to present trends in the underdeveloped countries.

Figure 1   Three-stage model of the demographic transition.

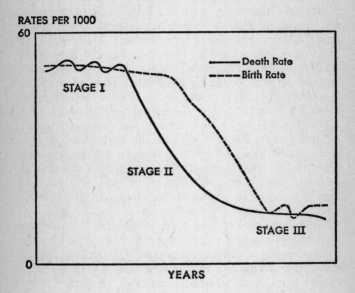

RATES PER 1000

1. That western Europe before the industrial revolution was characterized by a stable pattern of high fertility and mortality resembling the pattern observed in some contemporary underdeveloped areas is an assumption that has been challenged by recent work in economic history.[15] It now appears that fertility in premodern Europe was markedly lower than in Asian and African countries today, the result of a family organization centered on the married pair rather than on the consanguineal kin group, combined with a relatively indiv-

idualistic system of land tenure.[16] Moreover, population densities were far lower in Europe in the eighteenth and nineteenth centuries than they are in contemporary India, China, and southeast Asia, so that greater expansion of numbers was possible without threatening levels of living and controls achieved over mortality.[17] Another contention of transition theory that has been questioned is that declining mortality combined with stable fertility created the "demographic gap" permitting rapid population growth. A number of writers have argued that increases in fertility resulting from more frequent marriage and a decline in the age at marriage played a significant part in European population growth, although the evidence is by no means definitive.[18]

2. Detailed studies of the population history of particular countries reveal marked differences in the trend of their vital rates and considerable deviation from the generalized model of demographic transition.[19] Even those countries which conform to a full transition from high levels of fertility and mortality to low levels with an intervening period in which mortality decline was responsible for rapid growth show variations in the timing and duration of the successive stages of evolution that cannot be predicted from the generalized model. Almost as many countries are exceptions to the model as conform to it.

3. Crucial differences between contemporary underdeveloped countries and pre-industrial Europe have become increasingly apparent. Not only are population densities far higher in the former, but mortality has already declined in a number of non-Western countries far more rapidly than it declined in western Europe in the nineteenth century, when population growth was at its maximum. By adopting public health practices and medical technology developed by the advanced industrial nations of the West, contemporary underdeveloped nations can bring about a dramatic lowering of mortality in a far shorter period than comparable

declines occurred during the Western demographic
transition, when a fledgling medical science had, in
contrast to the effects of economic progress, little influence on mortality levels until the latter part of the
nineteenth century.[20]

This brief survey of evidence suggests that the broad
model of the demographic transition represents little
more than one possible pattern of population change
to which some Western countries have conformed in
the course of their industrialization. In view of the possible uniqueness of the circumstances under which
western Europe experienced economic and demographic
expansion, the three-stage model of demographic transition may have more in common with such concepts as
the "Renaissance," the "Reformation," and the "Bourgeois Revolution" than with logically precise scientific
generalizations. The demographic transition comes close
to Max Weber's "ideal type" characterization of a
"historical individual": an effort to summarize conceptually the broad pattern discernible in a complex
set of events—a pattern, however, that has no necessary predictive implications for events occurring in
another time and place and that does not even fully
describe the particular case from which it is generalized.

Perhaps this is too harsh a judgment. One causal
generalization of a trans-historical character appears to
be at least implicit in transition theory: the contention
that human populations are more readily inclined to
adopt innovations that will lower their mortality than
innovations that will lower their fertility.[21] If this is true,
mortality decline may always be expected to precede
fertility decline in societies undergoing economic development. Yet even this statement, which is based on
assumptions about universal human motives and values,
needs qualification and has little predictive utility. As
van Nort has pointed out, totalitarian governments may
elect to withhold from their subjects medical and public
health improvements requiring planned mobilization of

material and human resources.[22] Perhaps if the subjects were given a realistic opportunity to choose, they would give higher priority than their rulers to reforms improving health and longevity, but they may not be given this opportunity. Totalitarian governments are distinctive precisely because of their capacity and frequent disposition to ignore, even for long periods of time, the immediate demands and interests of their subjects.

Nor can the possibility be ruled out of governments adopting a policy of deliberately raising the death rate in order to reduce not population growth but existing overpopulation. Man-made famines and genocide are already firmly established in the repertory of twentieth-century politics. Hannah Arendt is one of the few political thinkers to have recognized this danger. In *The Origins of Totalitarianism,* she contends that rapid population growth in the huge, overcrowded countries of Asia has created hordes of "superfluous" people who constitute an ever-present temptation to resort to the precedent of political mass murder.[23] And, indeed, a continuation of the pressures of rapid growth is bound to heighten the appeal of totalitarian techniques as a form of drastic demographic surgery.

More generally, the very awareness on the part of governments, whether totalitarian or not, in underdeveloped and modernizing countries of the role played by population growth in hindering or facilitating economic development is likely to lead to efforts to manipulate deliberately the components of population growth in such a way as to preclude the unplanned and "automatic" demographic transition that took place in the West.

Yet whatever the theoretical status of the concept of the demographic transition, the change in the Western world since 1650 from a regime of high fertility and mortality to one of low fertility and mortality has been a major event in the history of mankind. Whereas fluctuations in the death rate have been the main determinants of population change in premodern societies, the trend of the birth rate, acutely responsive to changing social, economic, and cultural conditions, has become the key to future growth in the advanced industrial countries. The new demographic balance made possible by this development is immeasurably less wasteful both of human lives and of material resources than the high births-deaths balance that has existed through so much of human history and that still prevails over much of the earth's surface.

The Next Century

If a century from now we were to add an extra column to Table 1 showing the distribution of the world's population in 2060 and its growth since 1960, we can be reasonably certain that the history of the past century would not be repeated. While new technical and social inventions could conceivably reverse present trends, the growth of Europe and North America will undoubtedly be slower in the next century and that of South America and Africa faster. The area of greatest uncertainty is Asia. If the new Asian nations can make the transition from high to low levels of fertility and mortality that Europe achieved in the nineteenth and twentieth centuries, their populations may become stabilized at a size only slightly larger than at present. If they cannot alter their growth patterns in time, they may experience extremely rapid growth only to be faced ultimately with drastic increases in the death rate resulting from mass famines, epidemics, and wars. Because their future is today inextricably intertwined with ours, the uncertainties of their demographic outlook make all long-range forecasts of world population growth and distribution exceedingly hazardous. And, of course, the occurrence of a world-wide thermonuclear war would make the whole problem of estimating future trends on the basis of present growth patterns an utterly irrelevant undertaking.

Mortality

Social Attitudes Towards Death

Health and long life tend to be universal goals both for individuals and for social groups.[1] Conflicts between the individual's desire to implement these goals for himself and the social necessity of maintaining population are likely to be rare, in contrast to those areas of conduct where individual desires and the claims of society require delicate balancing and compromise. The situations in which conflicts do arise are of considerable sociological interest: societies on occasion demand the supreme sacrifice of life itself on behalf of group goals while continuing morally to censure suicide as a resolution to purely personal problems. Durkheim's famous distinction between "altruistic suicide" and other types of suicide is based on recognition of this difference.[2] Groups may possess sufficient power to sanction and carry out the involuntary killing of some of their members as in capital punishment, infanticide, or, on a mass scale, genocide. Groups with power may also deliberately withhold the means of maintaining life or health from others and develop ideological justifications for doing so.[3] Thus in practice individuals and groups often sacrifice life and health to other values.[4]

Yet after all these qualifications have been made, it remains broadly true that individuals rarely need elaborate cultural inducements to stay alive and that societies strive to maximize the survival chances of their populations. History amply attests to this, even though the notion of a specific self-preservation instinct is open to both logical and empirical objections.[5] Societies therefore tend to respond favorably to new ideas and practices, including those that have been scientifically tested, which promise to improve health and longevity. They are also apt to react less favorably to practices which promise to lower fertility but which inevitably violate deep-rooted mores governing sexual activity and reproduction and which interfere with long-established kinship institutions.[6] These rather abstract and schematic generalizations constitute the part of the theory of demographic transition that can with greatest justification lay claim to universal validity.

The population history of the Western world and of those Western nations that have undergone partial modernization reveals a more rapid decline in mortality than in fertility under the stimulus of economic advancement and medical progress. Death rates in western Europe, North America, and Australasia are already so low that only an actual lengthening of the life span—a scientific fountain of youth—could lower them much further. Medical advances have played the major role in bringing about the great reduction in Western death rates, while economic improvements have been more important "as permissive elements than as precipitating factors." [7] The diffusion of the latest discoveries of Western medical science to the underdeveloped countries has already permitted a rapid lowering of their death rates in the absence of the general economic advancement that preceded medical progress in the West. Thus the range of variation in levels of mortality throughout the world is far narrower today than in the last century and is conceivably narrower than it has ever been.

Death Rates: Trends and Differentials

In mentioning death rates, we have been referring so far only to what are called *crude death rates:* the annual number of deaths in a population per 1000 (or some other standard figure) of the total population. While the crude death rate in conjunction with the crude birth rate is a necessary measure for computing the natural increase of a population, it has serious inadequacies in a comparison between the mortality experience of two different populations, because it fails to take into account possible differences in their age composition.

People die in greater numbers at ages over forty, so an aging population may for this reason alone have a higher crude death rate than a population with a high proportion of young adults, even though health conditions in the former may be superior. This situation, in fact, is very frequently observed, for precisely those countries which have made greatest progress in reducing mortality have the oldest populations. In 1951, for example, the crude death rates of Jamaica and of the United Kingdom were 12.1 and 12.6 (per 1000) respectively. It would be quite erroneous to infer from these figures that levels of living and health conditions were slightly better in Jamaica than in Great Britain: the Jamaican crude death rate is lower than the British solely because of the former's younger population.

This is shown by comparison of the *age-specific death rates* of the two nations, that is, the number of deaths per 1000 persons in each specific age group rather than in the total population, the base for the crude death rate. To compute age-specific death rates, death registration certificates must, of course, include the age of the deceased. Usually specific death rates are computed for men and for women by five-year or ten-year age groups. Because of heavier mortality in the first year or two of life, death rates of children under five are ordinarily computed for one-year age intervals. The *infant death rate* measures mortality in the first year of life and is computed by relating the number of deaths under one year of age to the annual number of live births, rather than to the average number of children in the population at this age.

Comparison of age-specific death rates in Jamaica and the United Kingdom shows that in every age group the Jamaican rates are higher than the equivalent British rates for the same age groups—indisputable evidence of superior health and living conditions in the British Isles. Yet the British crude rate is slightly higher than the Jamaican because persons over forty are proportionately more numerous in the United Kingdom and mortality at these ages is higher than at lower ages.

Figure 2 shows the pattern of age-specific death

Figure 2   Relationship of age to death rate among the total population of the United States, 1900 and 1950.

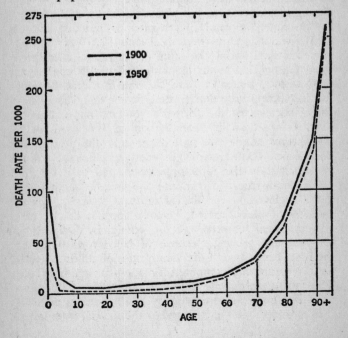

rates in the United States for 1900 and 1950. The rates form a lopsided U-shaped curve. In the first year of life, mortality is high; after the age of one it drops precipitously, reaching its lowest level at the beginning of the teen ages; from age ten to age forty the curve rises very gradually, but after forty its rise accelerates rapidly as the limits of life expectancy are approached. The difference in the shapes of the 1900 and 1950 curves reflects the differential gains made in reducing mortality at specific ages in the past half-century. Because of great gains in the reduction of infant mortality, the 1950 curve resembles a J more than a U. The similarity of the two curves for age groups over ten indicates lesser reductions in mortality at these ages, although some progress has been made since 1900 among persons of all ages.

Unfortunately, owing to deficiencies in the registration of information on the characteristics of the deceased, age-specific death rates cannot be computed for most countries outside of western Europe, North America, and Oceania. The most backward and isolated countries of the world have undoubtedly failed to make the progress that the United States had achieved as long ago as 1900. Other non-Western countries, profiting from cultural contacts with the West, have borrowed public-health techniques which have sharply reduced their mortality levels, especially their infant death rates, even though these countries have yet to undergo the industrial transformations that were associated with similar declines of mortality in western Europe and the United States.

Table 3 shows the crude death rates and infant death rates of a selected group of nations in 1930 and in 1965. The accuracy of some of the rates, particularly those shown for underdeveloped countries, is open to considerable question. The crude death rate is computed by relating the annual number of deaths to the estimated total population at the middle of the calendar year, so

it is affected by inaccuracies in both the registration of
deaths and in estimates of the midyear population.

The range of crude death rates for 1965 in the table
is from 6.0 for Japan to 16.8 for Guatemala. Crude
rates of 6-9 per 1000 are found only in exceptionally

Table 3   *Crude Death Rates and Infant Death Rates in Twenty
Selected Countries, Around 1930 and 1965*

Country	Crude Death Rate		Infant Death Rate	
	1930	1965	1930	1965
Argentina	11.4 ('38)	8.3 ('64)	96.6 ('34)	60.0 ('64)
Australia	8.6	8.8	47.2	20.5
Bulgaria	16.2	7.9 ('64)	138.3	32.9 ('64)
Canada	10.7	7.5	89.3	24.7 ('64)
Chile	24.7	11.2 ('64)	234.4	114.2 ('64)
Egypt	24.9	14.8	151.0	118.6 ('63)
France	15.8	11.1	78.2	22.0
Guatemala	24.7	16.8	83.9	94.6
Hungary	15.5	10.7	152.5	38.8
India	24.8	12.9 ('63–'64)	180.0	77.6 ('63)
Israel	9.5	6.2	68.5	27.3
Italy	14.1	10.0	105.5	35.6
Japan	18.2	6.0 ('64)	124.5	18.5
Mexico	26.6	9.5	131.6	64.5 ('64)
Netherlands	9.1	8.0	50.9	14.4
Portugal	17.0	10.3	143.6	64.9
Spain	16.5 ('32)	8.7	117.5 ('32)	37.2
Sweden	11.7	10.1	54.7	12.4
United Kingdom	11.7	11.5	63.1	19.0
United States	11.3	9.4	64.6	24.7

SOURCE: United Nations, *Demographic Yearbook, 1951,* Table 14, pp. 198-205,
and Table 19, pp. 328-335; *Demographic Yearbook, 1965,* Table 41, pp. 722-729,
and Table 42, pp. 730-740.

youthful populations and it is exceedingly doubtful
that death rates can be reduced below this level. Indeed they are likely to rise in the next few decades as

populations grow older. Aging alone accounts for the rise in the Australian rate in the period from 1930 to 1965. The rates for France and the United Kingdom are higher than those for the Netherlands and the United States primarily because the former have older populations. A death rate much below 12 to 15 per 1000 is a temporary phenomenon which cannot be maintained by a population with a balanced age structure unless its life expectancy is increased to over one hundred years of age.[8]

The crude death rates of the advanced urban-industrial nations in Table 3 fall roughly within a 9 to 12 range. In the less developed nations the range is about 12 to 17. Crude rates over 20 indicate especially poor health and living conditions. The actual rates for some of these high mortality countries may well be closer to 30 or 40 per 1000, rates which were quite common in western Europe in the eighteenth century.

The 1965 rates for most of the countries in Table 3 are lower than their 1930 rates, indicating that gains in the reduction of mortality have been world-wide in the present century. Declines have been proportionately greater, however, in those countries where the death rate is still high, the low-mortality countries having already reduced their death rates to a point where further improvements in public health and medicine are likely to be counterbalanced by the higher mortality rates of an aging population.

The infant mortality rate has been called "the most sensitive index of social welfare and of sanitary improvements which we possess." [9] It is clearly a purer measure of the socioeconomic and technological conditions determining mortality than the crude death rate, for unlike the latter, it is not affected by age composition. The range of the infant death rates shown in the last column of Table 3 is much wider than the range of crude death rates in the third column of the table—from a low of 12.4 for Sweden to a high of 118.6 for Egypt. In high-mortality countries, actual, as distinct from recorded, infant death rates over 200 are probably not uncommon. Rates of this magnitude existed in the Netherlands and Italy less than a century ago, a fact which highlights the very rapid progress made by Western nations in cutting infant mortality.[10] Gains made in the initial period of life far exceed reductions in mortality at more advanced ages.

The Life Table and Life Expectancy

The most complex instrument used by demographers to analyze mortality is the life table, which serves also as the basis for the actuarial calculations of life insurance companies. A bulky volume would be required to discuss the many uses of the life table and the mathematical details of its construction. We shall confine ourselves to a brief and unavoidably oversimplified description and an account of the most common measures of mortality derived from the table.

The life table is a method of summarizing the mortality experience of a single generation or cohort that is subject throughout its lifetime to a set of constant age-specific death rates. Starting with a set of age-specific death rates prevailing in a particular year (such as those for the United States in 1950 shown in Figure 2) or the average rates over a period of years, the life table tells us how many of 100,000 newborn babies will still be alive at each successive age if the selected age-specific rates are applied to them.

The life table does not, however, describe the experience of any actual cohort of live births, for age-specific rates vary from year to year, particularly in modern countries where, as we have seen, they have for some time been declining steadily. For instance, the age-specific death rate for persons aged twenty to twenty-four which prevails in the year of birth of a particular individual will almost certainly differ from the rate prevailing when he attains his twentieth birthday. The life table is based on the first rate rather than on the second, so it does not record what the actual mortality experience of a real cohort is likely to be. It describes rather the experience of a hypothetical cohort subject to a set of age-specific rates differing from those which actually determine the history of a real cohort as it matures, ages, and dies. To put it another way: *if* the rates at which persons in each age group die in a given year were the rates at which members of a single cohort, born at the same date, died as they passed through each successive age group in living out their lives, *then* the life table would describe the mortality history of a real cohort. Because of the variability from year to year of the age-specific rates, this is not the case. Nevertheless, the purely hypothetical nature of the mortality experience recorded in the life table does not debar it from providing us with several extremely useful indices of actual mortality conditions in a real population.

The life table assumes an initial population of 100,-000 live births. As mortality takes its toll, the survivors who reach each successive year of age dwindle in number until by the one-hundredth year only a tiny remnant of the original 100,000 is still alive. The number of survivors at any given age is, of course, a function of mortality in the preceding age groups. The life table for males in the United States in the years 1949 to 1951 reveals that as late as the seventieth year half of the original 100,000 would still be alive in a population subject to the age-specific rates of this three-year period.

Information of this kind illustrates vividly the manner in which mortality gradually but inexorably reduces every cohort of births. But its major importance is that the *average expectation of life* at any given age can be derived from it. The expectation of life at age forty, for example, tells us the remaining number of years that will on the average be lived under current mortality rates by persons reaching their fortieth birthdays. In effect, it measures mortality in the age groups after forty.

Table 4 *Life Expectation at Birth, Age 20, and Age 60 in Selected Countries at Specified Periods, Males and Females*

Country	Period	Age in Years					
		0		20		60	
		M.	F.	M.	F.	M.	F.
Australia	1953-1955	67.1	72.7	54.7	60.0	15.4	18.8
Canada	1960-1962	68.3	74.1	51.5	56.6	16.7	19.9
England and Wales	1841	40.2	42.2	39.9	40.8	13.5	14.4
	1881-1890	43.7	47.2	40.3	42.4	12.9	14.1
	1920-1922	55.6	62.9	45.8	49.9	14.4	16.5
	1961-1963	68.0	73.9	50.4	55.8	18.5	23.1
France	1795	23.4	27.3	36.5	39.4	13.1	15.7
	1877-1881	40.8	43.4	40.4	42.4	13.2	13.6
	1920-1923	52.2	56.1	42.9	46.2	13.8	15.6
	1963	67.2	74.1	49.7	56.1	15.5	19.6
Guatemala	1949-1951	43.8	43.5	41.1	40.3	14.7	14.3
India	1891-1901	23.6	24.0	31.7	28.6	9.5	10.0
	1921-1931	26.9	26.6	29.6	27.1	10.2	10.8
	1951-1960	41.9	40.5	37.0	35.6	11.8	13.0
Japan	1899-1903	44.0	44.8	40.3	41.1	12.8	14.3
	1926-1930	44.8	46.5	40.2	42.1	12.2	14.7
	1963	67.2	74.1	49.7	56.1	15.5	19.6
Netherlands	1900-1909	51.0	53.4	45.7	51.0	14.7	15.5
	1953-1955	71.0	73.9	53.7	60.8	17.8	18.9
United States	1929-1931	57.7	61.0	46.9	51.5	14.6	15.9
	1949-1951	65.5	70.1	48.9	58.5	15.7	18.5
	1963	66.6	73.4	49.5	55.6	15.7	19.6
U.S.S.R.	1958-1959	61.0	72.0				
U.S.S.R. (European)	1926-1927	41.9	46.8	43.2	47.3	14.8	17.1

SOURCE: All figures before 1900 are from W. S. Woytinsky and E. S. Woytinsky, *World Population and Production: Trends and Outlook*, New York: Twentieth Century Fund, 1953, p. 182; the other figures are from United Nations, *Demographic Yearbook, 1957*, Table 24, pp. 558-573; *Demographic Yearbook, 1961*, Table 24, pp. 622-650; *Demographic Yearbook, 1965*, Table 23, pp. 620-622.

Table 4 shows the average expectation of life at birth, at age twenty, and at age sixty for various nations at different dates in the past two centuries. Measures for both sexes are shown, because life tables are usually constructed for each sex separately in view of differentials in their mortality rates at most ages. The table contains a wealth of information, but we shall confine ourselves to brief comment on a few of its more salient features.

Note first of all that the range of differences in life expectation, whether between nations or between periods for the same nation, is far greater at birth than at age twenty or age sixty. In fact, at age sixty the range is not very wide at all. Life expectation at birth reflects infant mortality and it is at infancy that modern nations have made the greatest gains in reducing mortality. Progress in eliminating the diseases of middle age has been far less rapid. The contrast between conditions in high- and low-mortality countries is therefore most sharply revealed by the life expectation at birth figures.

These figures bring out strikingly the superiority of the nations of Western civilization. On an average, Americans and Englishmen live nearly thirty years longer than Indians and Guatemalans. Lack of necessary data prevents the construction of life tables in many backward countries, but the Indian experience is probably representative of other poverty-stricken agrarian populations. At the end of the eighteenth century, life expectation in France was about the same as in India in 1930 (Table 4). Clearly the gains in reducing mortality that nations such as India can anticipate if and when they complete their demographic transitions are very great.

More frequently than not, the life expectancy of women appears to have exceeded that of men at most ages, as Table 4 indicates. Men usually engage in more strenuous and dangerous occupations and thus expose themselves more often to the risk of injury and death.

Women, on the other hand, face the risk of death and debilitation in childbirth; in countries where modern medical care is still a rarity, female death rates in the childbearing ages are usually higher than male rates. In the more industrialized countries, however, deaths in childbirth have been so greatly reduced by antisepsis and obstetrical skill than even in the childbearing ages women have lower death rates than men. The superior longevity of women is greater in the more advanced countries than in the underdeveloped areas and has increased markedly in the past half-century. India and Guatemala, the two underdeveloped countries included in Table 4, are also the only two countries showing greater longevity for males at all or most of the ages for which rates are shown. A comparison of the size of the female advantage in France and England at the earliest and latest dates shown in the table reveals the trend towards an increasing differential favoring women.

Yet the fact that even at the earliest dates available for Western countries women were more long-lived while in contemporary underdeveloped areas men have a small advantage suggests that sex differentials in life expectancy may be caused by factors other than male occupational risks and maternal mortality. Possibly the traditional lower status of women in many non-Western populations lowers their survival chances by comparison with men, and the association of economic development with rising status of women reverses and progressively increases a sex differential favoring women in nations undergoing modernization.[11]

Nevertheless, even in infancy male death rates are usually higher, a fact that cannot entirely be explained by differences in the status of the two sexes. And an even more striking fact is that male stillbirths, even among foetuses gestated for less than three months, are more common than female stillbirths.[12] Since the sex ratio at birth almost universally favors males, greater female resistance to mortality may stem in part from unknown biological causes.

Two words of caution about the interpretation of measures of life expectancy are necessary. First, it must not be forgotten that they are derived from life tables, which are based on highly impermanent age-specific death rates. Thus American males that were born in 1963 will on the average live somewhat longer than the 1963 life table value of 66.6 years, because, barring some catastrophe, the age-specific rates prevailing in 1963 are higher than those rates which will actually determine their chances of dying through the greater part of their lives.

Second, the expectation of life at birth must not be confused with the *life span*. The latter is the number of years that the human species is hereditarily capable of surviving. Since the ideal conditions that would permit an individual to live out his absolute maximum potential have never existed, it is impossible to determine the exact limit of the life span. It is certainly higher than the biblical three score and ten years, for this figure equals the present average expectation of life in several of the more advanced contemporary countries.

"Expectation of a long life," Frederick Osborn has written, "is the most tangible end product of western European civilization. . . . Beside this gift the material things of our civilization seem insignificant. Who would exchange 30 years of life for all the automobiles, radios, television sets, telephones, or even all the bath tubs in the United States?" [13]

Causes of Death

As mortality has been brought under greater control, the relative importance of different causes of death has changed. Some diseases have been almost entirely eliminated by medical progress. Vaccination, for example, has reduced deaths from smallpox to the vanishing point in all regions with access to the resources of modern medicine. Malaria and typhus are other former scourges which are easily brought under control by preventive medicine. Their elimination from areas where they were formerly endemic has made a leading contribution to the world-wide decline of mortality in recent decades.

In the United States in 1900 the ten leading causes of death were, in order: tuberculosis, pneumonia, diarrhea and enteritis, diseases of the heart, nephritis, accidents and violence, cerebral hemorrhage, cancer, bronchitis, and diphtheria.[14] In 1964 the leading ten were: diseases of the heart, cancer, cerebral hemorrhage, pneumonia, accidents (both motor vehicle and other), diabetes, diseases of infancy, birth injuries, congenital malformations, and cirrhosis of the liver.[15] Tuberculosis and pneumonia alone, both infectious diseases, accounted for over one-fifth of all deaths in 1900, but in 1964 they contributed only about a twentieth of the total. Of the ten leading causes in 1900, two, diarrhea and enteritis and diphtheria, were primarily diseases of infancy. Their disappearance from the list by 1964 reflects the great gains made in controlling infant mortality in the past half-century. The major causes of infant mortality today are birth injuries and congenital malformations, neither of which is readily preventable. Conversely, five of the leading causes of death in 1964 are diseases characteristic of middle and old age: diseases of the heart, cancer, cerebral hemorrhage, diabetes, and cirrhosis of the liver. Together they account for over three-fifths of all deaths.

The accuracy of the recording of deaths by cause in the more backward countries leaves much to be desired, as the high rates for deaths from "senility" and "all other diseases" suggest. Omitting these residual categories, the ten leading causes of death in 1964 in Chile, a partially modernized country, were: pneumonia, cancer, infectious and parasitic diseases, diseases of the heart, gastritis and enteritis, accidents (both motor vehicle and other), cerebral hemorrhage, infections of the newborn, tuberculosis, and cirrhosis of the liver. Measles closely followed cirrhosis of the liver as a cause of death.[16] This list more closely resembles the list for the United States in 1900 than in 1964. Note the greater prominence of diseases peculiar to infancy and infectious diseases. In some of the even more backward countries of Africa, Asia, and South America, endemic infectious diseases such as sleeping sickness, cholera, and malaria undoubtedly still account for a large proportion of deaths. As early as 1900 in the United States, and by 1964 in Chile, considerable reduction in mortality at the younger ages had already been achieved, with the result that deaths from degenerative ailments such as heart disease, cerebral hemorrhage, and cancer, which are apt to develop late in life and which modern medicine has not yet succeeded in conquering, represent a large proportion of total deaths.

Future Trends in Mortality

Mortality levels in Western countries are already so low that further reductions equal in magnitude to those achieved in the past century are impossible. The complete conquest of cancer would merely be followed by rises in the death rates for other degenerative diseases that strike people at ages close to the limits of life expectancy.

Yet there are population groups in most Western nations whose mortality levels remain considerably above the national average. In the United States death rates for Negroes of both sexes are higher than the rates for whites, at all ages under sixty-five. The average expectation of life at birth for the American nonwhite population—mostly Negro—lags some seven or eight years behind that of the white population. Similar lags are found among urban slum dwellers and in the poorer rural areas of the United States and other modern nations. Some time will pass before these groups are brought up to the national average; future declines in their mortality will make a minor contribution to continued Western population growth.

The greatest changes in mortality levels in the immediate future are likely to occur in the underdeveloped countries. As indicated in the previous chapter, the rapid mortality declines in some of these countries since World War II raise grave doubts about the relevance to their situation of generalizations based on the past experience of the Western world. Western societies created their own mortality-depressing agencies in the form of scientific medicine and planned public health programs in the later stages of a process of economic and technological progress achieved over a period of a century and a half. Some of the most important discoveries of Western medical science have been made very recently. "The primary role of international rather than national health agencies, the use of antibiotics, the development of cheap yet effective methods for combating malaria—each of these is very nearly a midcentury innovation." [17]

But once these means of mortality control have been developed, non-Western countries can borrow and apply them without undergoing the thorough transformation of their social and economic structures that took place in the West. Relatively simple public health measures such as spraying crops with insecticide or incinerating refuse have sharply reduced mortality in some areas, although these practices have been imposed from the outside and have produced no fundamental modifications of the social structure. The most dramatic instance is the case of Ceylon, where the death rate dropped by 34 per cent in a single year, 1946-1947, largely as a result of malaria control achieved by the spraying of fields with D.D.T. There is no recorded instance of so rapid a drop in any Western nation.[18]

Mortality fell most rapidly in Western countries in the late nineteenth and twentieth centuries, and the decline was largely the result of medical progress in disease control. In the eighteenth century it was probable that, as a contemporary remarked, "more people perish at the hands of doctors than are cured by them." [19] Not until the discoveries of Semmelweis, Jenner, Pasteur, and Koch in the middle and late nineteenth century did the influence of progress in medical science begin to be felt in the economically advanced countries of the West. Before this period the long secular decline in mortality was largely due to economic improvements such as increasing agricultural efficiency, the introduction of superior varieties of crops and livestock permitting better diets, and improvements in transportation eliminating famines due to local food shortages.

The fact that the far more rapid mortality declines in underdeveloped areas have resulted from the importation of Western medical techniques which have not been independently developed as part of an over-all social and economic modernization raises questions about their permanence. People may be saved by modern medicine from infectious diseases and yet die of starvation. The greatest gains in mortality control in the West were achieved after the birth rate had begun to decline; the achievement of even more rapid gains where habits of high fertility persist and birth rates have long been higher than they were in the pre-industrial West intensifies a population pressure that is already a primary cause of the poverty and economic backwardness of many non-Western areas. Unless these areas can make the transition to industrialization and low levels of fertility in time, the recurrence of famine and ensuing social and political unrest may not only prevent further declines in mortality but may even wipe out the gains that have already been made.

Fertility

Social Determinants of Fertility

Both the human desire to remain alive and the desire to procreate and thus prolong the life of the species are often regarded as relatively uncomplicated biological drives so obvious as to require no further analysis. This proposition is doubtful even as regards individual self-preservation, as was indicated in the previous chapter, but it is far more questionable when applied to procreation. The high incidence of voluntary celibacy and child-lessness in many societies, the great variability of fertility levels and preferences among social groups, and the decline in Western birth rates in the past century largely owing to the deliberate intentions of millions of parents, all suggest that the intensity of the desire to procreate is a highly uncertain quantity. It appears to be far more uncertain and variable than the desire for sexual gratification by means of coitus, which, although a prerequisite for procreation, gives rise independently to cultural regulations restricting and channeling it. In contrast to mortality, the motivations and social norms governing reproduction are exceedingly elaborate and variable.

Sometimes it is maintained that only modern Western populations fail to procreate to the limit of their natural capacity. Primitive and agrarian peoples are assumed to reproduce like subhuman species, biological impairments and geographical barriers alone interfering with their fertility. Voluntary control over fertility is certainly more widespread and effective in contemporary

Western societies than in other populations of the past or present, but fertility is socially controlled to some extent in all populations. Even where the controls are not imposed and maintained for the express purpose of limiting fertility, cultural norms and kinship institutions, even in the most backward preliterate societies, prevent the full realization of *fecundity*, the maximum biological capacity for reproduction, which is to be distinguished from *fertility*, or actual reproductive performance.

Physiologically, women are capable of bearing children between the ages of about fifteen and forty-nine. Allowing for periods of sterility following childbirth, the average human female is probably capable of bearing as many as fifteen or twenty children, excluding multiple births, but in no known human population have all fecund women, or even the great majority, averaged so many offspring. Thus there is a gap between the total fecundity and the actual fertility level achieved in all populations, although individual women may often approximate biological capacity in their childbearing performances.

All the social factors influencing fertility, whether intentionally or unintentionally, must obviously impinge upon the reproductive process, that complex series of physiological events beginning with sexual intercourse, requiring the union of sperm and ovum that constitutes conception, and terminating with successful gestation of the foetus and childbirth. In a useful article, Kingsley Davis and Judith Blake have classified the social variables affecting fertility according to the stages of the reproductive process that they influence either by interfering with or by facilitating its completion.[1] The social variables are grouped under three main headings: factors affecting exposure to intercourse, factors affecting exposure to conception, and factors affecting exposure to gestation and parturition (birth). The first group, the "intercourse variables," includes age of marriage or of entry into sexual unions, frequency of permanent celibacy of females, length of time spent after or between sexual unions during the woman's reproductive period, amount of voluntary and involuntary sexual abstinence, and frequency of intercourse. The second group of factors, the "conception variables," includes involuntary fecundity or infecundity, contraceptive usage or nonusage, and fecundity or infecundity as affected by voluntary practices such as sterilization and medical treatment. The third group of factors, the "gestation variables," includes voluntary and involuntary abortion. Infanticide may also be regarded as a means of controlling fertility, although it appears on the mortality side of the births-deaths ledger.

Some of the "intercourse variables" have a minus effect on fertility in all populations, for no known society permits coitus between any and all biologically capable partners on any and all occasions. The cultural regulation of sexual conduct is universal, although sex mores vary widely in detail. Most societies lie somewhere between the extremes of a high tolerance of nonincestuous sexual unions and the proscription, never fully successful, of all premarital and extramarital coitus. Some societies forbid intercourse between husband and wife for specific periods after childbirth or during periods of religious observance. Various classes of persons, such as priests, may be required to remain celibate. Premarital intercourse is often proscribed in societies where the customary age at marriage for women is several years after puberty, with the result that unmarried women make no contribution to the fertility of the population in spite of their physiological capacity to do so. The prohibition of widow remarriage in societies with low male life expectancy ensures that many women will remain infertile just at the time when they are living through their most fecund years. The widespread institution of monogamous marriage combined with the prohibition of extramarital coitus necessitates the infertility of one mate if the other happens to be sterile;

"thus the very institutions which are devoted to procreation (marriage and the family) are in part checks on fertility."[2]

When Davis and Blake distinguish between "voluntary" and "involuntary" factors affecting fertility, they mean simply those that either are or are not subject to control in a given society relative to its knowledge and resources. It should not be inferred that voluntary practices influencing fertility have been instituted and maintained for that purpose. The lower fertility resulting from the effects of sexual regulation is often an unintended consequence of practices that are justified on religious, moral, or socially pragmatic grounds. The need to avoid illegitimacy, or unmarried parenthood, is a paramount consideration: many societies, unlike our own, dissociate coitus and parenthood and are highly permissive of the former so long as it does not lead to births out of wedlock.[3] On the other hand, particularly in advanced societies, controls over sexual conduct may originate and survive for deeper social and psychological reasons having little to do with the connection between sex and procreation.[4] This consideration is often overlooked by sexual reformers who argue rationalistically that the invention of effective contraceptive methods removes all social necessity for restraints on sexual freedom, while the sociological rationale for such restraints is a minor consideration to alarmed moralists who condemn birth control precisely because it permits the separation of sexual pleasure from procreation and thus removes one of the supports of restrictive sexual mores that these moralists value for their own sake.

In contrast to many of the voluntary practices classed by Davis and Blake as intercourse variables, the voluntary practices included in the conception variables and the gestation variables represent deliberate efforts to influence fertility. Contraception by whatever means, sterilization, the medical treatment of sterility and infecundity, and induced abortion clearly are ways in which individuals, with or without social approval, intentionally prevent or encourage fertility.[5] Most of these are ways of limiting or preventing fertility. Yet, as Davis and Blake observe:

> One cannot say, as is frequently implied in the literature, that some of these variables are affecting fertility in one society but not in another. *All* of the variables are present in *every* society. This is because . . . each one *is* a variable—it can operate either to reduce or to enhance fertility. . . . In other words, the absence of a specific practice does not imply 'no influence' on fertility, because this very absence is a form of influence. It follows that the position of any society, if stated at all, must be stated on all eleven variables.[6]

This consideration suggests the necessity of giving as much attention to the ways in which societies encourage childbearing as to the ways in which they limit it. The former are, in fact, usually much more direct and explicit. When conditions of high mortality are present, only those populations which succeed in inducing their members to procreate frequently will successfully perpetuate themselves. Since the vast majority of human societies have suffered from high mortality, variants of the biblical injunction to "be fruitful and multiply" are part of the value systems of most cultures. Social organization based on enduring kinship units; the granting of special economic, political, and religious privileges to parents; permitting sexual enjoyment only to the married; the stigmatization of celibacy and childlessness—all these promote favorable attitudes to fertility and encourage frequent and early marriage and childbearing. Moreover, they induce unfavorable attitudes toward practices impeding fertility such as sexual abstinence, contraception, abortion, and infanticide. Most pre-industrial societies, long subject to high mortality and with social structures organized around kinship ties, have strong, built-in supports maintaining high fertility. The precipitous decline of death rates in underdeveloped areas in recent decades without a corresponding transformation of their social structures is the main cause of the world-wide population explosion in the present century.

The fertility of a population depends, therefore, on the balance between those parts of its culture and social system that favor reproduction and those that hinder it. Study of the motivations and social determinants underlying fertility variations is inescapably a task for the sociologist, because reproductive behavior is a form of motivated human conduct resembling the other types of motivated conduct that he investigates.

Birth Rates: Trends and Differentials

The most commonly used measure of fertility is the *crude birth rate,* the annual number of births per 1000 (or some other standard figure) of the total population. Like the crude death rate, it is an inadequate index for many purposes because it fails to take into account the age and sex composition of the population. The preponderantly male populations of frontier regions such as Alaska show very low crude birth rates, yet the few women in the population marry early and give birth to numerous children. Since only women between the ages of approximately fifteen to forty-nine can bear children, changes in the proportions of women at these ages will affect the crude birth rate even if the average number of births per woman stays the same.

The effects of age-sex composition can be held constant by relating births to the number of women of childbearing age rather than to the total population. Such rates are usually called *general fertility rates.* Births out of wedlock make up an insignificant proportion of total births in most societies, so the computation of rates only for married women of childbearing age

provides a still more accurate measure of female reproductive performance. The calculation of *age-specific
marital fertility rates* adds a further refinement.

Until the "baby boom" of the 1940's and 1950's, the
crude birth rates of Western countries declined continuously for over half a century. In the majority of
them the decline began in the 1870's. Table 5 shows
the crude birth rates in each decade from 1801 to 1965
of a number of modern nations.

Table 5   *Crude Birth Rates, Selected Countries, 1801 to 1965*

Period	Sweden	France	Switzer-land	England and Wales	United States
1801-10	30.9				
1811-20	33.4	31.8			
1821-30	34.6	31.0			
1831-40	31.5	29.0	32.9		
1841-50	31.1	27.4	30.8	32.6	
1851-60	32.8	26.3	29.8	34.1	
1861-70	31.4	26.3	31.4	35.2	
1871-80	30.5	25.4	30.7	35.4	37.0[a]
1881-90	29.1	23.9	28.1	32.5	
1891-1900	27.1	22.2	28.1	30.2	29.8[b]
1901-10	25.8	20.6	26.7	27.2	27.7[c]
1911-20	22.0	15.3	21.0	21.8	24.2[d]
1921-30	17.5	18.8	18.5	18.3	23.5
1931-40	14.4	15.5	15.8	14.8	17.2
1941-49	18.7	17.6	19.0	17.1	20.0
1950-54	15.3	19.5	17.3	15.5	24.4
1955-59	14.5	18.4	17.5	16.0	24.6
1960-64	14.5	18.0	18.5	17.9	22.4

[a] 1871-75.   [b] 1896-1900.   [c] 1907.   [d] 1915-20.
SOURCE: Paul H. Landis and Paul K. Hatt, *Population Problems*, Second Edition,
New York: American Book Company, 1954, p. 159; United Nations, *Demographic
Yearbook*, 1965, Table 12, pp. 276-299.

With the exception of France, where fertility began
to decline early in the nineteenth century, the birth rate
in all of the nations listed in Table 5 remained over 30

per 1000 until the final decades of the century. It fell to its lowest point in France in the decade of World War I and in the other countries in the decade of the Great Depression. An upturn of the birth rate in the 1940's occurred in all five nations. Their experience is broadly representative of that of other Western nations conforming to the type 5 growth pattern discussed in Chapter 2.

Table 6 *Crude Birth Rates, Selected Countries, 1911–1913, 1930–1934, 1940–1944, 1950–1954, and 1960–1964*

Country	1911-1913	1930-1934	1940-1944	1950-1954	1960-1964
Argentina	37.4	26.8	24.1	25.0	22.4
Bulgaria	35.8	30.3	22.1	21.7	16.9
Ceylon	36.5	37.8	36.6	38.5	34.9
Chile	39.9	40.5	36.4	33.8	34.8
Egypt	42.3	45.4[b]	39.6[c]	43.8	42.8
Guatemala	41.2[a]	51.6	47.2	51.4	47.4
India	38.6	45.2[d]	39.9[e]	41.7[f]	38.4[g]
Italy	31.7	24.5	20.8	18.4	21.8
Japan	34.1	31.8	30.1	23.7	17.2
Mexico	31.9[a]	44.5	44.2	45.1	46.0
Spain	27.5	27.5	22.0	20.3	21.6

[a] 1921-25. [b] 1930. [c] 1944. [d] estimate for 1931-1941. [e] estimate for 1941-1951.
[f] estimate for 1951-1961. [g] estimate for 1963-1964.
SOURCE: United Nations, *Demographic Yearbook, 1951*, pp. 146-147; *Demographic Yearbook, 1965*, pp. 276-299.

Table 6 shows the birth rates of eleven nations, all of which have lower standards of living and most of which are considerably less industrialized than the nations listed in Table 5. The rates for Chile, Egypt, Guatemala, Ceylon, India, and Mexico, all nations belonging to growth types 2 or 3, have not declined at all between 1911-1913 and 1960-1964. In Argentina, Bulgaria, Italy, Spain, and Japan, representative type 4 countries, the birth rate has fallen more rapidly than in western European countries and the United States over the same period. The fertility differentials between countries in different stages of the demographic transi-

tion are even more marked than the mortality differentials that were summarized in the previous chapter.
A comparison of the crude birth rates shown in Table
6 with the crude death rates shown for some of the
same countries in Table 3 indicates the enormous gap
between births and deaths and the resulting high rates
of natural increase currently existing in some underdeveloped areas.

In the period from 1911 to 1913 all the less advanced countries had birth rates which were as high as
or higher than the birth rates of the western European
countries in the 1830's or 1840's. By 1964 the majority
of the former countries show birth rates approximately
equal to those of the United States and western Europe
at the beginning of the twentieth century. In other
words, a difference of about fifty years of demographic
evolution separates the two groups of countries. Today a
crude birth rate of over 30 can be considered very high,
one of 20 to 30 moderately high, and one of less than
20 suggests a recent history of fertility decline.

The Measurement of Family Size

The phrases "fall of the birth rate" and "decline in
family size" are often used interchangeably, but they
by no means refer to the same thing. The birth rate is
based on all births occurring in a given year; it is a
measure of current fertility. By family size, however,
demographers mean the total number of children born
to a married couple over the whole of the wife's reproductive span. Declining family size is, of course, reflected
in the trend of the birth rate, which is the justification
for loosely considering the two as interchangeable; but
for purposes of more detailed demographic analysis
they should be distinguished. As we have noted, the
birth rate is affected by changes in the proportions of
married women and of women in the reproductive age
groups. Such changes have played little or no role in

the long-run decline of the birth rate in the Western world, which has been almost entirely the result of changes in family size, but in the short run, as we shall see in greater detail when discussing the recent baby boom, changes in marriage rates have made a sizable contribution to fluctuations in the birth rate.

Direct information on changes in family size can be acquired from census data on the number of children ever born to married women in various age groups. Questions on the number of children ever born have been asked of wives in the censuses of several countries and are a major source of our knowledge of fertility behavior. From the answers, the *average family size*, that is, the average number of children per woman, can be computed. If the information is also requested, the average family sizes of women who married at particular ages or particular dates can also be calculated. It is important to distinguish between the *completed* families of women who are past the childbearing ages and the *incomplete* families of women under forty-nine who may still bear additional children. The average size of the family is sometimes called the *cumulative birth rate*, which may be defined as all births occurring to a given group of women from the date of marriage to the end of the childbearing period per 1000 women in the group.

In England the average size of the completed families of married women who were born in 1841-45 and were questioned at the 1911 census was just under six children, whereas that of women born in 1861-65 was somewhat less than five.[7] The difference between the two figures tells us more precisely than the crude birth rate what was happening to fertility in the last decades of the nineteenth century. English women who married in 1900-09 showed an average completed family size of slightly more than three children in 1946, while the generation that went to the altar in 1925-29 bore an average of only two and a fraction children.[8] The change

from an average family size of nearly six in the Victorian
era to two in the 1930's and 1940's is a striking one.
Similar changes have occurred in other Western countries.

Changes in average family size, however, do not tell
us whether the change is due to an increase in child-
lessness (no-child families), a decline in the number
of very large families, an increase in small families
combined with a decline in middle-sized families, or a
combination of two or more of these together. Data on
the distribution of all families by size are required to
give us this information. Table 7 shows such distribu-
tions for English women marrying in the middle of the
nineteenth century and in 1925. It gives a clearer picture
of the shift to small families than either the crude birth
rate or measures of average family size. The difference
between the two cohorts of women is marked and
reveals the changes in family size preferences underlying
the trend of the crude birth rate. As the British Royal
Commission on Population of 1946 pointed out:

> The Victorian families are well spread out over the
> various sizes of family, all the numbers of children up
> to 10 being substantially represented; in modern times
> there is a heavy concentration on the smallest families.
> . . . The proportion of childless couples has about dou-
> bled; the proportion having only one child has risen five-
> fold since the nineteenth century and the proportion
> having 2 children fourfold. At the other end of the scale
> the proportion of couples having 10 children or more
> has been reduced from 16 per cent to less than 1 per
> cent.[9]

The experience of England and Wales may once again
be regarded as generally representative of that of the
United States and other Western countries.

Some direct information about the trend of family
size can be gained from current birth rates when information on the number of children previously born to
each mother is obtained on birth registration forms.

Table 7 *Changes in the Distribution of Families by Size,
Great Britain*

Number of Children Born	Marriages Taking Place About 1860 (England and Wales) Per cent	Marriages of 1925 (Great Britain) Per cent
0	9	17
1	5	25
2	6	25
3	8	14
4	9	8
5	10	5
6	10	3
7	10	2
8	9	1
9	8	0.6
10	6	0.4
Over 10	10	0.3

SOURCE: Royal Commission on Population *Report*, London: His Majesty's Stationery Office, 1949, p. 26.

Such data tell the same story: there has been a steady decline in the rate for fifth and all higher-order births.

Causes of the Western Decline in Family Size

The decline in the fertility of Western populations is a social phenomenon of unmistakable significance. This decline has been attributed to almost everything under the sun, even to spots on the surface of that astral body. Far-reaching historical changes such as the purported "Decline of the West" and trivial habits of modern life such as bicycle riding, which has been reputed to have a harmful effect on the female reproductive organs, have been invoked to explain it.[10] Today population students generally agree that the decline is owing to voluntary causes, that it is, in effect, the result of

deliberate restrictions on procreation consciously practiced by modern populations.

Voluntary and Involuntary Causes   Common sense
and the evidence of personal experience have long suggested this, but there have nevertheless been many
writers, and there are still a few today, who have given
greater weight to involuntary causes. Some have argued
that the fecundity of modern populations has declined
and have sought for evidence of greater female sterility.
Others have emphasized the unintended effects on
fertility of modern habits and customs: The nervous
strain of modern life which, it is alleged, lowers the
intensity of sexual energies and thus reduces the frequency of intercourse, dietary changes, and the greater
use of soap, an effective spermicide, are among the
causes advanced as possible explanations of the fall in
family size.

The evidence with respect to loss of fecundity is
conflicting. Advances in medicine and the extension of
medical care to more people have increased our ability
to diagnose infecundity, so one cannot conclude any
more than in the analogous cases of psychoses and
numerous other pathologies that an actual increase in
incidence has taken place. Biological explanations of
the decline in the birth rate are inherently unconvincing
in view of the rapidity with which it has fallen; changes
in genetic reproductive capacity great enough to account
for the downward trend would probably require several
generations, yet the decline was manifest within a much
shorter period. New habits possibly conducive to lower
fecundity and fertility may have played a minor role,
but one can also find contemporary customs and conditions favorable to higher fecundity and fertility, such
as greater leisure, more adequate diets, and better
obstetrical care.

In short, it is hard to see how involuntary causes
could have made more than a minor contribution to

the decline in family size. As the British Royal Commission concludes, "the alternative view, that the decline in family size has been brought about wholly or mainly by deliberate family limitation, is far better supported."[11]

The Advantages of Small Families　The desire for a higher standard of living is the chief single consideration which has induced people to restrict the size of their families. In an industrial market economy a financial outlay is required to obtain goods and services, and the rising expenses of bearing and rearing children must compete with other demands on the family budget. Family limitation allows people to enjoy the social and sexual pleasures of married life without undergoing the physical and economic hardships of raising numerous children. Urban living has made it difficult to accommodate large families in cramped living quarters, and the decline in the relative number of family farms and business enterprises has reduced the value of a large family as a source of unpaid labor.

Many writers of the previous century, drawing inferences from Malthus' famous theory that he himself declined to make,[12] thought that higher standards of living would encourage larger families, but they have had precisely the reverse effect. In part this is because more comfortable material circumstances have made people less willing to undergo the privations of bearing and rearing families of from five to ten children, but a more important reason is that the very social and economic changes which have raised Western standards of living have also created a wider economic gap between parents and nonparents. Bringing up children has for most people involved a reduction in their standard of living.

Other changes favoring smaller families have occurred: the partial emancipation of women from the eternal drudgery of childbearing and housework, the increase in divorce, the decline in the solidarity of the

family group, the breakdown of rigid moral and religious codes governing family life which has permitted
rational calculation to exercise greater influence on
fertility behavior, to mention only a few of them. All
of these changes are interrelated and are involved in the
transformation of a predominantly rural and agricultural
society into a society organized around city living and
industrial production.

Why did the decline in the birth rate begin in so
many countries just when it did in the eighth decade
of the nineteenth century after many of the basic changes
of the industrial revolution had already taken place?
Probably the fall in family size actually started several
decades earlier in some population groups, especially
among upper- and middle-class city-dwellers who were
the first to experience the benefits of a rising standard
of living. Not until the latter part of the century did
the practice of family limitation spread to the urban
working class, a pattern of cultural diffusion down the
class hierarchy which has often been observed in the
case of other, quite different folkways.

The Role of Birth Control Moreover, the 1870's
witnessed a great increase in the dissemination of contraceptive information and improved mechanical techniques of contraception. The latter were more effective
means of limiting family size than abortion or "folk"
methods such as *coitus interruptus,* the rhythm method,
and crude mechanical techniques, all of which had been
known in western Europe since at least the medieval
period, though perhaps not as widely as in earlier non-
Christian civilizations. The invention of the vulcanizing
process of rubber in the 1840's made possible large-
scale production of cheap rubber contraceptives, but not
until several free-speech court trials gave widespread
publicity to the propaganda of birth control advocates
did contraceptive knowledge spread rapidly among the
less educated segments of the population. Their acquisi-

tion of this knowledge coincided with the spreading impact of the social changes favoring small families.

Sometimes the fall of the birth rate is explained entirely as a consequence of the improvement and increased dissemination of contraceptives and contraceptive knowledge. Yet sheer knowledge of a technique and its easy availability are not enough to induce someone to make actual use of his knowledge. He will do so only if the technique serves definite pre-existing needs. Contraceptive knowledge has clearly been a major means of limiting family size, but the causes of fertility decline must be sought in the emergence of attitudes favorable to smaller families.

Moreover, recent studies have shown that the role of mechanical and chemical contraceptives has often been overestimated: rhythm and *coitus interruptus* are still widely used forms of birth control in Western countries, notably in France, and by working-class couples in other nations.[13] Abortion, which was legalized in Japan in 1948, has become a major means of family limitation in that country, contributing to the rapid decline in the Japanese birth rate in the 1950's from its high level in the immediate postwar period. What little evidence there is on the frequency of abortion in Western countries indicates that married women most frequently resort to it.

These facts suggest the possibility that the instantaneous abolition of all mechanical and chemical contraceptives would not necessarily be followed by a sharp upswing in the birth rate. So well established is the preference for smaller families in modern society that older more burdensome methods—or others—would probably be substituted for contraception. No doubt some increase in unwanted pregnancies would occur, but it might be counteracted by greater sexual abstinence and later marriage.

The transition from a way of life in which few restrictions were imposed on fertility to a new era of birth control in which having children has become subject to voluntary choice is a momentous one. Many of the deeper motivational changes involved have been ignored in the above account. There is some evidence that the upper classes of earlier civilizations deliberately restricted family size after marriage, but only in the urban-industrial societies of the modern world has planned parenthood been practiced by the mass of the population.

Recent Trends in Western Fertility

In most Western countries, birth rates, which had fallen to their lowest recorded levels during the world depression of the 1930's, rose slightly toward the end of the decade as nation after nation slowly recovered economically. Short-run fluctuations of the birth rate had occurred before in the course of the long decline in fertility. But to the surprise of most population students, birth rates continued to rise in several nations during World War II, and in the immediate postwar period the entire Western world, with the exception of war-ravaged Germany, experienced a resurgence of fertility which carried birth rates to levels well above those of the 1930's. More surprising still, they have remained at levels higher than those of the thirties into the sixties, although there have been declines from the postwar peaks. This phenomenon has been popularly called the baby boom. Since it is the first clearcut reversal of the fertility trend since the decline of the birth rate began in the nineteenth century, its long-range significance has been widely debated.

In the 1930's there was widespread concern over the falling birth rate and many people, including some population students, jumped to the rather sweeping conclusion that modern society was by its very nature inimical to reproduction. Some popular writers have passed equally broad judgments on the subsequent rise of the birth rate, proclaiming that it represents a departure from the small-family system and a revival of the values associated with domestic life. Demographers, chastened by their failures of prediction in the previous decade, have avoided final assessments and have concentrated on sharpening their tools of demographic measurement in order to understand precisely what has happened to upset the past trend. In doing so, they have become more aware than ever before of the limitations of the trend of the crude birth rate as a true indication of changes in fertility behavior.

We have seen that the long decline of the birth rate was primarily the result of a spreading preference for small planned families. In the short run, however, other factors affect the rate which have played a leading role in the baby boom. The birth rate will rise if fewer women remain unmarried, if the proportion of women marrying at early ages and thus exposing themselves to the risk of childbirth for a longer period increases, if the proportion of childless marriages declines, and, finally, if women space their births differently over the childbearing period, bearing their first children sooner after marriage than previously.

All these things have happened since the late 1930's and none of them involves a return to the larger families of the past. A decline in childless marriages will, of course, raise the average family size of married women, but a decision by more married women to have one or two children rather than none at all hardly constitutes a new preference for large families. The effects of changes in the spacing of births are of particular interest. Family limitation makes possible not only the planning of family size, but also control over the spacing and timing of births. Married couples can postpone having a child when economic conditions are not propitious, or alternatively decide to have their children soon after marriage and close together when conditions are favorable. Changes in the spacing and timing of births may produce fluctuations in the birth rate without any changes occurring in the size of completed families.

If depression brings about the postponement of marriages and births, prosperity encourages both the making up of the postponed marriages and births of the preceding depression period and the moving ahead of marriages and births which might otherwise have occurred at a later date. Economic circumstances favorable to family-building may also induce people who might otherwise have remained single to marry and people who might otherwise have remained childless to have children. All these things may happen in the absence of any trend towards an increase in the proportion of large families.

There may also be long-run trends in marriage rates, the average age at marriage, and the spacing of childbearing after marriage that are relatively independent of fluctuations in economic circumstances due to the business cycle. Such trends may lead to a rise in measures of *current* or *period fertility*, such as the crude birth rate, in the absence of any pronounced trend toward larger families.[14] Measures of *cohort* or *longitudinal* fertility showing the total childbearing performance through time of groups of women born in the same year are needed to determine precisely what is happening when the birth rate shows an upward trend as in the period of the postwar baby boom.

The size of completed families cannot be known until women are past the reproductive period. Since many of the women who contributed to the postwar baby boom are still in the reproductive ages, we will not know for some time whether there has been any increase in the average size of completed families which were started at the end of the war. The baby boom has not reversed the long decline in the rate for births over the fifth child, but the continuing decline in large families may be sufficiently countered by the decline in childlessness and an increase in medium-sized families to produce a slight increase in the average size of completed families.

However, as Ansley J. Coale observes, referring to the United States: "Recent cohorts have been setting twentieth-century records at each stage they pass. We have no apparent assurance that they won't continue to set records through the higher birth orders. In other words, cohort analysis indicates that the baby boom *may* connote only relatively moderate increases in completed size of family, but such an inference is permissive, not obligatory." [15]

Although all Western nations experienced a postwar rise in current fertility, it was more pronounced in some countries than in others. In all of them it appears to have been primarily due to higher rates of marriage, earlier ventures into both marriage and parenthood, and declines in childless and one-child marriages.[16] However, in the United States, Canada, Australia, and New Zealand, but also to a lesser extent in the older western European nations of France and Finland, a trend towards slightly larger families among families with more than one child appears to have taken place.[17]

Since 1960 the birth rate has declined by 22 per cent in the United States. Young couples are both marrying and having their first child somewhat later than in the peak baby boom years of the 1950's. The rapid adoption in the past five years of anti-ovulant pills as a form of contraception undoubtedly has some bearing on the recent decline in American fertility.[18] It is too early to tell if the decline will continue, but the postwar baby boom seems, in any event, to have ended.

In contrast to attempts to explain the earlier long downward trend of Western birth rates, there is not even room for doubt that the reversal of the trend is due to voluntary causes or that it reflects positive decisions concerning marriage and childbearing by groups which had previously learned to control their fertility. Although an understanding of the precise nature of the link between economic conditions and fertility behavior requires analysis of partially independent cultural and psychological factors, one can say that the postwar baby boom in the West took place during a period of prosperity and increased economic security beneficial to all groups and that this was at least a necessary condition for its occurrence.

Fertility in Nonindustrial Societies

Many sociologists and population students believe that the birth rate in countries undergoing urbanization and industrialization will eventually decline as their citizens come to prefer small families for substantially the same reasons that led Westerners to do so. The experience of Japan, the one non-Western country to achieve full economic and demographic modernization, supports this belief.[19] Yet the values and reproductive institutions of nonindustrial peoples are by no means alike, and their impact on the trend and pattern of fertility in the course of the modernization process may vary accordingly.

It is often assumed that formal religious teachings are a major influence encouraging early marriage and high fertility in nonindustrial societies. Yet, although of all the world religions Christianity has been the most doctrinally hostile to family limitation, it is in the Christian West that family planning, largely by contraceptive means, has been most widely adopted despite the opposition of church and secular authorities as well. The official values of a society as expressed in its sacred books and legal codes may be less important in affecting reproductive behavior than family organization, cultural definition of sex roles, and other social facts that endure at a level "below" the expressed value systems and the frequently changing religious teachings. The Roman Catholic Church condemns "artificial" birth control more resolutely than any other contemporary

Christian or non-Christian religious body; in some Catholic populations the Church's influence is a major factor maintaining high fertility, but in others where the population is both Catholic and highly fertile, nonreligious factors are more important than religious ones. A number of studies have shown, for example, that the nominal Catholicism of most of Latin America has little to do with the high birth rates—the highest recorded in the world—prevailing in that region. Male association of virility with numerous children, female sexual prudery, and lack of communication on sexual and reproductive matters between husband and wife have been far more influential in sustaining high fertility than Catholic opposition to family planning programs, an opposition which has in any case abated in recent years.[20]

The joint or extended family system of most Asian cultures is an institutional arrangement strongly conducive to high fertility.[21] Economic deterrents to early marriage and childbearing are absent when married couples are free from sole responsibility for both their own and their children's care and support as a result of their residence in a large household that includes other adults and holds land and economic assets on a common rather than an individual basis. The obligation under strongly patrilineal systems of descent and inheritance to produce a son, wide tolerance of polygynous marriage or concubinage, the low status of women limiting the emotional intimacy between husband and wife required for effective contraceptive usage, and the frequent segregation of unmarried women preventing premarital sexual contacts that might provide motivation for birth control, are other institutional factors favoring early marriage and early and frequent childbearing in Asian cultures, whether they are Moslem, Hindu, or Buddhist in religion.

Many of these conditions were absent in pre-industrial Europe in spite of Christian pronatalism and sexual asceticism. Pre-industrial Western civilization, with its roots in classical and Hebrew culture, always placed greater responsibility on the nuclear family. The married couple was expected to establish an independent household (neo-local residence), ownership of land was individual rather than collective, rules of descent and inheritance were less unilineal, thus reducing the obligation to bear sons to carry on the patrilineal line, and the status of women was higher, subtly affecting the intimacy of the marriage relationship and permitting greater premarital contacts between the sexes that provided opportunities for sexual relations and experimentation with birth control techniques. In his famous advocacy of the "prudential" postponement of marriage as a check to population growth, Malthus was simply reasserting a disapproval of early, economically irresponsible marriage that had long existed in the West and had its roots in the family and property system.

The reproductive institutions of the pre-industrial West, therefore, appear to have encouraged late marriage, "folk" methods of family limitation, and relatively moderate fertility long before the industrial revolution. Vigorous Christian opposition to abortion and infanticide, which were common in classical times, may have led to greater reliance on delayed marriage and birth control after marriage as means of checking fertility. The spread of family limitation by contraceptive means and the preference for small families that accounted for the decline of the birth rate in the late stages of the industrial revolution possibly represented an intensified revival of fertility controls that had always been part of Western culture.

Such a view suggests that it would be rash to assume that contemporary Asian countries will simply repeat the "unplanned" fertility decline that occurred in the West. Government action and the support of other institutional authorities may be necessary to overcome that resistance to small families and family limitation which is rooted in the joint family system and the low status of women.[22] The contrast between the effects on fertility of Eastern and Western reproductive institutions, however, is only one of several considerations indicating that purposeful population policies may be required to facilitate the modernization of contemporary underdeveloped areas.

But what about Japan? This question can never be ignored in the comparative study of economic and demographic change. Like other Asian cultures, traditional Japan also possessed a patrilineal joint family system, a religion that favored high fertility, and sex role definitions according women a status far inferior to that of men. Yet Japan successfully completed the process of economic and demographic modernization. Irene Taeuber, however, reports considerable evidence that fertility control, largely by means of abortion and infanticide, was widely practiced in pre-industrial Japan of the Tokugawa period.[23] A major difference between the traditional social structures of Japan on the one hand and of India and China on the other was the presence in Japan of "other aspects of social organization that could override the family." [24] Significantly, the historical record reveals "only two fully proven cases of feudalism, those of western Europe and of Japan." [25] Thus in spite of kinship institutions similar to those of the rest of Asia, Japan also resembled western Europe in possessing the distinctive institutions of feudalism. Reischauer's observation may well be applicable to fertility patterns as well as to "political and economic forms":

> No one has ever clearly stated or carefully studied the general thesis that the feudal experience in Japan produced certain characteristics which were similar to some of the major characteristics of postfeudal Europe and that these points of similarity made it easier for the Japanese to adopt the political and economic forms of the contemporary West.[26]

Future Uncertainties

Thus in both the West and the East, though for different reasons, the future trend of the birth rate is in doubt. In the West marriage and birth rates no longer reflect deeply rooted customs and mores, or, as in the period of declining fertility, gradual adaptation to the spread of urbanization and industrialization. Control over the number and spacing of births enables people quickly to adjust their reproductive behavior to changes in their social and economic situation. Thus fertility no longer behaves like an independent variable but has become closely tied to economic conditions, world affairs, and cultural fashions, rising and falling (though within fairly narrow limits) in response to booms, depressions, wars and fears of war, and the possibly permanent changes in the social structure that result. In the East, birth rates still reflect the persistence of traditional reproductive institutions, but the fate of these institutions and the high fertility they sustain depends on the Eastern underdeveloped countries' ability to achieve the social and economic modernization of the West. The different fertility patterns of the East are one of the reasons for doubting facile extrapolations of earlier Western experience.

Two assertions by population specialists made twenty years apart aptly reveal the uncertainty with which future fertility trends are now regarded. In 1930 O. E. Baker wrote that "the population of the United States, ten, twenty, even fifty years hence, can be predicted with a greater degree of accuracy than any other economic or social fact, provided the immigration laws are not changed." [27] In 1952, Irene Taeuber wrote: "The answer to 'What will happen?' or even to 'What is probable?' is not to be found in the formal manipulation of population statistics. . . . The problem of the future of population growth is the problem of the future of the culture." [28]

Differential Fertility

The Significance of Differential Fertility

A population's birth rate, or any other index of its aggregate fertility, is clearly a measure that averages the fertility of the different social groups of which the total population is composed. Accordingly, such an over-all measure conceals fertility differences which may exist between these groups. Population students have long been interested in the differential fertility of groups smaller than entire national populations for three main reasons:

1. Study of the fertility of relatively small and socially homogeneous groups such as social classes enables the population student to isolate the determinants of reproductive behavior more easily than when he deals with such large and heterogeneous units as modern nations. Now that social and cultural factors operating through personal motivations are generally accepted as the main determinants of fertility, most recent research in differential fertility has sought to specify these factors more concretely by investigating groups with similar values and positions within their larger social structures.

2. The presence of certain group fertility differentials provides clues to the possible future trend of fertility in the whole population. Thus demographers studying populations which have not yet undergone modernization have sought to discover whether city-dwellers and the upper classes have lower birth rates than the rest of the population. If this proves to be so, and if urban-

ization and industrialization are proceeding rapidly, they may conclude that the low fertility patterns of the upper classes are likely to spread from the cities and down the class hierarchy to a widening segment of the total population.

3. Fertility differences between groups distinguished by social or biological criteria determine the proportions of the total population which these groups will constitute in the future. If Group A is more fertile than Group B, the descendants of persons in Group A will clearly increase their representation in the total population at the expense of descendants of persons in Group B. Most of the pioneer studies of differential fertility were made by biologists and geneticists who feared that the higher fertility of the lower classes would result in progressive deterioration of the biological quality of the population. This alarmist view that differential fertility starts a process of "gene erosion" in the population raising the threat of eventual "race degeneration" has declined in recent years, in part because of the spread of a sociological outlook minimizing the importance of genetic determinants of human behavior, and in part because of the narrowing of the major group fertility differentials themselves in Western populations.

Differential fertility studies have for the most part been confined to the largest and sociologically most important subdivisions of national populations: size of community, occupation, education, income, social class, religion, race, and national origin. These groupings obviously overlap in varying degrees. One of the main methodological problems of differential fertility analysis is to isolate the effect on reproductive behavior of each group affiliation or social attribute considered singly.

Of the group fertility differences most frequently studied, religion, race, and national origin have been of relatively secondary importance in most Western nations. There have long been differences in the fertility of

Catholics, Protestants, and Jews, but co-religionists differing in residential (rural-urban) and socioeconomic status have not tended to resemble one another as closely in their fertility behavior as they resemble persons of the same status who differ in religious affiliation.[1] The main exceptions have been Western nations such as Belgium, the Netherlands, and Switzerland whose populations are fairly evenly divided along religious lines.[2] But even in these countries it is usually difficult to isolate the exact effects of religious affiliation as such, for religious differences tend to be correlated with residential and socioeconomic differences that independently affect fertility behavior. There are signs that in a number of Western countries, notably the United States, religious differentials are becoming a more important source of fertility variation than in the past in urban populations which have shown a marked narrowing of socioeconomic differentials in the last three decades.[3] Conceivably, such a result reflects a general tendency in mature industrial societies for traditional religious affiliations to retain considerable vitality and possibly increase in significance even when, and perhaps precisely *because,* other group differences—class, ethnic, and residential—have declined in importance.[4] Yet it needs to be remembered that the religious fertility differentials that investigators have uncovered are within a narrow range, and frequently it is *attitudes* towards childbearing rather than behavior that have been found to differ most markedly along religious lines.[5]

No evidence exists of differences in fecundity linked to racial traits. Differences in the fertility of ethnic and nationality groups reflect differences between their countries of origin, but they tend to vanish as immigrants become fully aculturated to their new homelands.[6]

In populations that are sharply divided along religious, racial, or ethnic lines fertility differences between such groups may be of considerable intrinsic interest.

Rivalry between groups may sometimes take the form of competitive efforts to encourage large families with a view to gaining ascendancy of numbers in the future. Yet the generalization that residential and socioeconomic characteristics have usually played a larger part in accounting for differential fertility is still justified.

Rural-Urban Differentials

The rapid urbanization of the Western world since the industrial revolution has been one of the major social changes bringing about lower fertility in modern populations. As a rule, fertility has been found to vary with the degree of urbanization; it is higher in rural than in urban communities, and in smaller than in larger urban aggregations. References to the large families of peasants and farmers as compared with those of townspeople are to be found in the writings of nearly all past civilizations. There is statistical evidence of the existence of a rural-urban fertility differential in Sweden as long ago as 1760.[7] In western Europe and the United States, a rural-urban differential existed throughout the nineteenth century and has probably been a feature of Western civilization for a much longer period, perhaps since the earliest cities and towns first came into existence.

Family limitation by contraceptive means originated in the cities. When it began to spread to the urban working classes in the late nineteenth century, the gap between rural and urban fertility widened. The surplus rural population was drawn off the land to the cities and contributed to their rapid growth. Rural populations are still more fertile than urban populations in all countries with large rural populations, but they too have participated in the downward trend of fertility in the present century, and their birth rates did not rise as much as those of the less fertile urban groups during the recent baby boom.

Class Differentials[8]

The higher fertility of the lower classes has been observed so often in so many different countries that the existence of a negative correlation between fertility and class or socioeconomic status has virtually acquired the force of a sociodemographic law. The correlation has long been a feature of Western civilization[9] and probably existed in the civilizations of antiquity as well. In nonindustrial civilizations, however, the upper classes constitute only a small proportion of the total population, so their lower fertility has little effect on the general fertility level.

The social and economic changes attending industrialization have given class fertility differentials greater demographic significance. Urbanization, the rise in the general standard of living, the emergence of large socioeconomic strata occupying a position intermediate between the top and the bottom of the class structure, and the increase in individual opportunities to climb the social ladder have led to the diffusion of family limitation from small groups at the apex of the social hierarchy to a growing proportion of the total population.

When the birth rate began to fall in the late nineteenth century, the negative relation between fertility and socioeconomic status became more pronounced. Family limitation was spreading among the urban upper and middle classes, but the working classes and country residents continued to raise large families. Until World War I, class birth rates diverged rapidly. Not only did the size of the fertility differential between classes increase, but the fertility of high-status groups declined at a more rapid rate than that of low-status groups. During this period, alarm was widely expressed over the ultimate consequences of the failure of the "best people" to replace themselves while the supposedly "biologically inferior" stocks were multiplying rapidly.

In the period between the two World Wars, however, the trend of class differentials was reversed in nearly all countries for which adequate data exist. While the fertility of all classes declined more rapidly than previously, lower-class birth rates fell faster than upper-class rates. The differentials between classes contracted in size, and the earlier diverging trend was replaced by one towards convergence. This shift of trend was observed no matter what indices of class position were used in the many studies of differential fertility made at this time. Some researchers used groupings of occupations ranked according to socioeconomic status; some selected educational level as an index of class; others used ecological criteria and compared the birth rates of "rich" and "poor" or "bourgeois" and "proletarian" urban districts.

Since 1945 another shift in the trend of class differentials has occurred. The relatively infertile high-status groups—professional men, businessmen, the college-educated—have participated to a greater extent in the post-war rise of fertility than the more prolific low-status groups of industrial workers, manual laborers, and those without any high-school education.[10] The fact that the least fertile segments of society showed the greatest increases was one of the most significant aspects of the baby boom. Class fertility rates converged as in the previous period, but differential rates of fertility increase replaced differential rates of decline.

The *trend* of class fertility differentials, then, has undergone changes since the early period of declining fertility, when class birth rates were diverging. What about the *pattern* of differentials? In general the negative relation between fertility and socioeconomic status has persisted, but exceptions to this relation are revealed if one uses more than a simple two- or threefold division of the class structure. White-collar, semi-professional occupations, and small businessmen—the main compo-

nents of what is often called the lower-middle class—
have in almost all Western countries been the least
fertile segments of society, exhibiting lower birth rates
than big employers, professionals, and other upper and
upper-middle class elements. For some countries differential fertility data are available only for broad socioeconomic strata, but it is usually possible to distinguish
at least between higher nonmanual, lower nonmanual,
nonagricultural manual, and agricultural occupations.
Invariably the lower nonmanual occupations prove to
be the least fertile socioeconomic stratum.

Farmers and agricultural workers are usually the
most fertile stratum. The rural-urban fertility differential is partly a concealed occupational class differential
between agriculturalists on the one hand and those
engaged in commerce, manufacturing, government service, the professions, and other urban occupations on
the other. The agricultural-nonagricultural differential
is still a large one in modern societies, although it too
has narrowed in recent decades. Within the farm population, a positive as opposed to a negative association
between fertility and socioeconomic status has often
been observed both in industrial and nonindustrial
societies, although it is more characteristic of the latter.

Figure 3 shows the trend of occupational class fertility differentials in the United States for thirteen successive cohorts of native white married women born between the late 1830's and the late 1890's. All these
women were past the reproductive ages at either the
1910 or 1940 censuses, when the total numbers of
children they had ever borne were recorded. The figure
reveals a widening of the class fertility differentials for
the earlier cohorts who bore their children in the latter
half of the nineteenth century. These cohorts also exhibit the greatest declines in fertility. The cohorts born
after 1875 show a less rapid fertility decline, and the
gap between their class fertility rates narrows slightly,

Figure 3   Cumulative birth rates by occupational class, native white once-married women of completed fertility, born between 1836-40 and 1896-1900, United States.

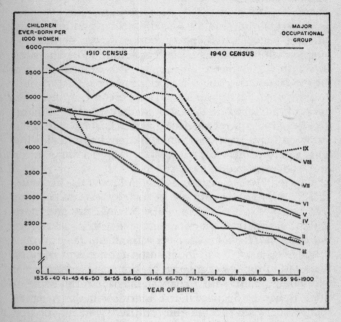

OCCUPATIONAL CLASSES

   I. Professionals and Semi-professionals
  II. Proprietors, Managers, and Officials
 III. Clerical, Sales, and Kindred Workers
 IV. Service Workers
  V. Craftsmen, Foremen, and Kindred Workers (skilled)
 VI. Operatives and Kindred Workers (semiskilled)
VII. Laborers, Except Farm and Mine (unskilled)
VIII. Farmers and Farm Managers
 IX. Farm Laborers and Foremen

SOURCE: United States Bureau of the Census, Sixteenth Census of the United States, *Population, Differential Fertility 1940 and 1910, Fertility by Duration of Marriage*, Tables 11 and 13.

at least for the nonagricultural occupations (Classes I-VII). The figure also shows the exceptionally low fertility of white-collar employees (Class III).

Income Differentials

Studies of how fertility varies with income level have also revealed a broad association between low income and high fertility, and vice versa. But the pattern of negative correlation between wealth and fertility is much less regular than that between occupational rank and fertility. The negative correlation usually holds in urban groups only up to the second or third highest income group, the highest groups having somewhat larger families than those immediately below them but failing to match the average family size of groups at the lower end of the income scale.

Data on income group fertility differentials, however, are not very meaningful, because income classifications cut across the distinction between manual and non-manual occupations and agricultural and nonagricultural occupations. Because farmers and farm laborers are usually the most fertile population groups and most of them fall in the lower income brackets, an income scale combining them with urban, nonagricultural occupations is likely to conceal irregularities in the negative relation between income and fertility.[11] The association between income and fertility, therefore, is more fruitfully examined when socioeconomic status is held constant, that is, *within* homogeneous occupational classes.

Among people of similar social class and occupational background, there is an inclination for those with the largest incomes to have larger families than their less prosperous fellows. This tendency is particularly true among urban, nonmanual workers, who, in several countries, show marked departures from the general pattern of decreasing family size with increasing income In the Scandinavian cities of Stockholm and Oslo, persons in the middle rather than at the upper end of the income scale had the smallest families in the 1930's.[12] An earlier Stockholm study demonstrated a positive correlation between income and fertility,[13] but no other studies have yet revealed so complete a reversal of the usual inverse relationship.

Interpretation of Differential Fertility

The Diffusion of Birth Control. Group differences in fertility are today largely the consequence of differences in the practice of family limitation by means of contraception. Differences in the average age of marriage, of considerably greater importance in the past, continue to play a minor part, the upper classes habitually marrying later than the lower classes.

The changes in the trend and pattern of group fertility differentials which have taken place in the present century reflect the gradual spread of family limitation through all layers of the population. The evidence supporting this interpretation was, until recently, largely inferential. The initial divergence of class fertility rates followed by their later convergence, the exceptionally low fertility of salaried white-collar workers (a group usually aspiring to a middle-class standard of life but earning comparatively low incomes), and the high fertility of rural groups isolated from the main currents of social change suggested that preferences for small planned families had slowly percolated down from the top to the bottom of the class structure.

Two studies of class differences in contraceptive practice have supplied direct evidence confirming this theory. Whelpton and Kiser's massive study of a sample of married women in the city of Indianapolis showed that effective planning of family size was more common among the less fertile upper-class wives.[14] Lewis-Faning's study of a large sample of British women showed that among women married before 1920, upper-class wives used birth control much more frequently than lower-class wives, but among women married between 1920 and 1935 there was little difference in the percentages of birth control users in each class.[15] Lewis-Faning also found that more upper-class women used the most effective appliance methods of birth control, although the percentage of lower-class women using these methods has steadily increased in the past three decades.

In addition to discovering that class fertility differentials were largely attributable to class differences in the practice of birth control, Whelpton and Kiser divided their sample into groups differing according to the degree of success with which they had planned the size of their families and then examined class fertility differentials *within* homogeneous family-planning groups.[16] The pattern of class differentials among successful family planners departed markedly from the customary inverse association between social status and fertility observed in the general population. Successful planners in the highest socioeconomic groups were almost as fertile as those at the bottom of the social scale. Planners of intermediate class status had the smallest families.

These findings have stimulated considerable discussion among students of differential fertility. They raise the possibility that if and when birth control becomes universally practiced, fertility may become positively correlated with socioeconomic status. Another possibility is that differential fertility may disappear altogether: fertility differentials among successful family planners in the Indianapolis sample were very small and revealed no consistent relationship between family size and class position. The small differentials in the Scandinavian countries suggest that birth control has been more widely adopted by all classes than in the United States or Great Britain.

We cannot assume, however, that the pattern of differential fertility exhibited by successful family planners in a population where contraception is still not

practiced by many lower-class groups will resemble the
pattern developing when large majorities in all classes
successfully plan the size of their families. Lower-class
planners today may be a group with special characteristics differentiating them from other members of their
class. They may, for example, be persons with strong
aspirations to improve their class position and a resulting disposition to spend a large part of their incomes on
conspicuous consumption than on children.[17]

It is largely in order to answer such questions that
population students have in recent years turned to new
methods and approaches in the study of fertility. The
outstanding development in recent fertility research has
been the use of survey and interviewing procedures
developed by sociologists to probe the values and motives related to contraceptive practices and family size
preferences. Since the traditional fertility differentials
associated with such broad social classifications as income, occupation, and residence have been narrowing,
interpretation of remaining sources of fertility variation
in the population has stressed such subtler and less
easily measurable traits as mobility aspirations, family-
centered attitudes, and feelings of personal adequacy.
The postwar baby boom, which took population students completely by surprise, has also encouraged closer
investigation of values and motivations which are both
partially independent of such broad characteristics as
occupation or residence and which at the same time
represent "intervening variables" explaining the link
between these characteristics and fertility behavior. The
most extensive of these newer studies, reflecting family
planning and fertility trends in the years since World
War II, strongly confirms earlier predictions that traditional fertility differentials would continue to narrow to
the point of virtual disappearance if and when family
planning spread to all groups in the population.[18] This
result lends support to the effort to explore the less
obvious, attitudinal determinants of fertility behavior.

Social and Psychological Factors The Whelpton-Kiser study of Indianapolis pioneered in the use of survey methods to explore social psychological factors in differential fertility.[19] Although its findings, summarized above, regarding the interrelations between family size, contraceptive usage, and socieconomic status were highly significant, the search for attitudinal correlates of family planning and fertility yielded rather disappointing results. The importance of socioeconomic status in accounting for fertility variations was confirmed, but the investigators were unable to find any decisive relationships, independent of socioeconomic status, between family planning and fertility on the one hand and such psychological variables as "liking for children" and "rationality of outlook" on the other.[20]

Several later studies have attempted to improve upon the methodology of the Indianapolis study and to employ larger and more representative samples of the national population.[21] These studies have greatly increased our knowledge of the extent of family planning in the American population, of the methods of contraception that are most widely used, and of the hopes and desires regarding family size of American couples. A major conclusion is that "a majority of white couples in all social strata do not have larger families than they want." [22] Moreover, there appears to be considerable consensus on the desirability of a two-to-four-child family throughout the American population, suggesting that with the spread of family limitation a common social norm governing family size has begun to crystallize.

Yet, in spite of their improved methodology and sampling range, these studies have not been much more successful than the Indianapolis study in isolating psychological factors related to fertility variation. Their main definitive finding has been that religion and education are of greater independent significance, at least in urban groups, than was formerly believed. Perhaps large-scale survey research, with its emphasis on the statistical manipulation of answers to standardized questionnaire inquiries about *attitudes,* is not adapted to uncovering the basic motivational determinants of *behavior* in such emotionally significant areas as husband-wife relations, sexuality, childbearing and child care, and family solidarity. A more subtle, qualitative approach, drawing upon the clinical experience and theoretical resources of psychiatry, appears to be desirable.

A few studies of differential fertility reveal a more sophisticated and systematic understanding of the motivational context of contraceptive behavior and child-bearing derived from psychoanalytic theory.[23] Yet only one of these, Rainwater's pilot study of a small sample of American working-class husbands and wives, is concerned with a population group in an advanced rather than an underdeveloped area. Comparing this study with the large-scale survey studies, a reviewer remarks:

> It emphasizes contraceptive *behavior* rather than attitudes towards contraception; it is aware of the complexity of the feelings involved in the reproductive process; and the most praiseworthy of all its meritorious qualities, it never forgets that fertility and family planning have something to do with sex and the unconscious. This relationship should be self-evident; yet, the fact of the matter is that it usually has been ignored in studies of American fertility.[24]

By means of long and searching intensive interviews, Rainwater and his associates discovered that fears and inhibitions about sex, and ignorance and mythological beliefs about the physiology of reproduction, the anatomy of the female sex organs, and the rationale for chemical and mechanical contraceptive devices are still widely prevalent in the American working class. Such attitudes and beliefs prevent effective use of contraception and are a major source of the undesired large families still to be found in this segment of the population. In addition to its superior insights into the motivational obstacles to family planning, this study also serves as a useful reminder that the middle-class groups which have been the chief focus of earlier studies may still differ strikingly from many working-class couples in their attitudes and achievements with respect to family planning.

If the survey method studies of differential fertility are limited by their inability to probe the deeper facets of motivation, the value and relevance of the investigation of psychological factors as such has also been challenged. Some critics have gone so far as to question the usefulness of any effort to explore the motives underlying fertility behavior as an unwarranted form of "psychological reductionism." [25] In this writer's view this extreme position is unjustified, although it may be granted that the survey studies have not always clarified the precise role attributable to psychological factors, and the rationale for these studies—whether their primary aim is interpretative understanding or the improvement of forecasts of future births—has not always been clear.[26]

A more moderate criticism is that studies stressing psychological variables are not well adapted to dealing with trends over time since we have no measures comparable to census and vital-statistics data on socio-economic characteristics indicating the distribution of psychological traits in the total population, either at the present or for earlier periods.[27] If, however, the psychological concepts employed are sufficiently "sociologized" by specification of their linkage to institutional patterns, a comparative sociology of reproductive institutions and their change through time may compensate for this defect.[28] Inquiries into the psychological attributes associated with high or low fertility are of greatest value when they are treated as supplementary to sociological analysis of the effects on the family and childbearing of the social and economic changes which have so profoundly altered the class structure and cultural outlook of Western societies in the past half-century.[29]

Migration

Migration as a Demographic Process

When any area smaller than the entire world is considered, migration must be taken into account as a possible influence on population size. Viewed as a demographic process, migration differs in important respects from mortality and fertility. Lacking a biological basis, it is neither inevitable like death nor, like reproduction, a prerequisite for the survival of the species. It is a more distinctively human activity. "Popularly we rank animals higher than plants in our hierarchy of cosmic phenomena because, unlike vegetables, animals normally are not attached to one spot." [1] What is true of animals is, with the possible exception of the great seasonal migrations of some species of birds, even truer of men. The motives for which men migrate are far more heterogeneous than their attitudes towards death or childbearing. "Like all human behavior, [migration] is rooted subjectively in psychological drives; objectively in conditions which stimulate those drives." [2] Several distinct types of migration characterize different kinds of social order. All they have in common is the movement of persons from one geographical area to another. Efforts to explain migration by postulating such psychologically universal drives as "wanderlust," or the action of external pressures upon man's innate "sitzlust," to employ a counter-concept facetiously coined by William Petersen, are even less satisfactory than the interpretation of mortality and fertility in terms of "self-preservation" and "procreative" instincts.[3]

The demographic causes and effects of migration are simply one element in a complex human experience and social process. The diversity of group and individual motives for migrating, the acculturation of migrants to the institutions of their new homelands, the individual and social disorganization they often experience in unfamiliar surroundings, the contributions they make to the way of life of the new communities in which they settle[4]—these are only a few of the topics examined by students of migration which often have little direct bearing on its significance for the study of population *per se*. Yet in order to understand fully the contribution migration may make to the size and distribution of population, the population student frequently has to take into account its qualitative and historically peculiar features. Although his interest necessarily tends to be even more selective than his interest in mortality and fertility, migration always occurs in a distinctive social and cultural context from which it cannot be separated.

Basic Definitions and Types of Migration

The term *migration* is commonly used generically by population students to designate more or less permanent changes of residence. Movement across an international boundary is usually called *external* migration to differentiate it from the more frequent *internal* migrations of persons within the boundaries of a single nation. *Immigration* and *emigration* are the names conventionally given to movements into and out of a nation respectively, while *in-migration* and *out-migration* are applied in a corresponding way to intranational population movements.

William Petersen has developed an elaborate typology of migration in an effort to improve upon earlier typologies that failed fully to take into account the many variables involved in the concrete movements of peoples.[5] He distinguishes five basic classes of migration: primitive, forced, impelled, free, and mass. Each class is subdivided into innovating and conservative types of migration. Migration is *innovating* when persons "migrate as a means of achieving the new"; it is *conservative* when they migrate in response to changed conditions in their homelands "in order to retain what they have." [6]

Primitive migration, in its conservative form, includes the wandering and ranging of hunting, food-gathering, and pastoral peoples, and, in its innovating form, "flight from the land," or the movement of nomadic and agrarian peoples to cities, the locus of a new urban way of life.

Forced migration refers to the compulsory transfer or displacement of peoples by the state, for example, the actions taken by the Nazi and Soviet governments with regard to Jews, Volga Germans, Tatars, and other groups they wished to destroy by genocide or to relocate. The slave trade constitutes an innovating form of forced migration.

Impelled migration differs from forced migration in that "the migrants still retain some power to decide whether or not to leave." [7] Flight before the advance of a stronger and more populous invading people, as in the "barbarian invasions" of Europe in the early Christian era, and flight before advancing armies in modern times, constitute conservative forms, while the coolie trade in Asia and the migration of indentured servants to the eighteenth-century British colonies constitute innovating forms. The refugee from racial, religious, or political persecution is an example of impelled conservative migration.

Free migration refers to individual movements, usually motivated by a search for novelty, adventure, or improvement. Free migrants are pioneers who pave the way for the later *mass* migration of entire groups once migration has become "a style, an established pattern, an example of collective behavior." [8] The most important recent historical example of mass migration has been the great overseas movements from Europe in the nineteenth century. In modern times these movements have been of greater demographic significance than any others. Mass migrations of groups to regions and communities resembling as closely as possible those they have left are a conservative form of migration, whereas movements of peasants and small farmers to cities as part of an on-going process of urbanization represent an innovating form.

In modern times the flow of international migration has largely depended on the tolerance of national states. Thus a further distinction is frequently made between *free* and *controlled* or *selective* migration, usually with the contrast between international migration in the nineteenth and twentieth centuries in mind.[9] Throughout most of the nineteenth century and until after World War I in the present century, the United States and other overseas countries settled by Europeans imposed few restrictions on immigration, but they have since departed from that policy. In the present century "the welfare of the national state has become, to one degree or another, the main criterion for judging whether migration is 'good' or 'bad,' " [10] with the result that all nations now regulate the numbers and kinds of people they will admit as immigrants. Totalitarian and authoritarian nationalist governments have also limited and regulated the numbers and kinds of people emigrating from their territories.

Migration Before the Modern Era

In early history most movements of peoples were undoubtedly group movements. In small preliterate tribal societies individuals rarely act independently of their clan or tribe. Before the invention of agriculture, food-gathering economies based chiefly on hunting and fishing provided subsistence, and entire tribes pursued a nomadic existence wandering in search of areas where food was abundant. Such wanderings were initiated by ecological pressures: the desiccation of lands, the retreat of icecaps, the occurrence of floods, and climatic changes. Their routes were largely determined by the permissiveness of geography: the navigability of rivers, the steepness of mountain ranges, the accessibility of fertile valleys, and the size and aridity of deserts. Fossil remains indicate that even the protohuman ancestors of *homo sapiens* were wanderers. It is now generally believed that the first true men originated somewhere in East Africa and ranged and wandered over a period of many centuries until all the major continents were occupied by human beings. Isolation and in-breeding led to biological differentiation into racial stocks, resulting in the distinctive geographical distribution of the major races with which we are familiar in the modern era.

The invention of agriculture and the birth of civilization (Childe's food-producing and urban revolutions) resulted in new, innovating forms of migration. The contacts of primitive food-gatherers and nomadic herdsmen with settled agriculturalists and city-dwellers were often violent, but were invariably culturally productive. Commercial and imperialist migrations were characteristic of the Mediterranean civilizations, which were themselves eventually inundated by "barbarian invasions" from the north. The movements of exiles, traders, mercenaries, and pilgrims frequently carried an awareness of urban civilization to isolated folk and peasant societies. Such individual movements, however, scarcely compared in volume or importance with the military invasions and group settlements that enabled the ancient civilizations and medieval Europe to extend the territorial scope of their influence.

Invasions by "barbarians" from the northern and

eastern borders of Europe, and by such civilized peoples to the east as the Arabs and the Turks, were a major part of the history of Western civilization until the twelfth century. The Crusades were one of several counter-movements to the east. In the tenth and eleventh centuries the voyages of the Norsemen to Greenland and America "provided the first hint of the coming importance of overseas migration." [11] After the discoveries of southern Africa and the New World of the Americas in the fifteenth and sixteenth centuries, transoceanic movements supplanted land invasions as the major form of migratory expansion. The African slave trade, the Spanish conquest and settlement of South America, and the establishment of British, French, and Dutch colonies in North America, Africa, and Australasia helped shape the world as we know it today.

International Migration in the Nineteenth Century

The nineteenth century and the first three decades of the twentieth were the heyday of free individual migration. They witnessed the most extensive mass movement of peoples recorded in history. With the greatest volume of movement across the Atlantic to the Americas, the distance covered by the migrants has also never been equaled. The great demographic expansion of Europe in the nineteenth century took place in two ways: by natural increase and by mass emigration to the relatively empty continents overseas.

Since 1800 there has been a total immigration of approximately fifty-seven million people to the Western Hemisphere of whom about thirty million, or over half, have entered the United States. The largest number of immigrants came to the United States between 1901 and 1910, when nearly nine million entered. The second largest number, over five million, arrived in the decade of 1881 to 1890. From 80 to 90 per cent of American immigrants came from Europe, although there have also been large movements from other countries in the Western Hemisphere, particularly from Canada. However, many of the inter-American migrants were themselves recent immigrants from Europe. French-Canadians moving across the border from Quebec into New England constitute the most important exception.

In the course of the nineteenth century, changes took place in the chief countries of origin of the immigrants to the New World. Until about 1880 the bulk of immigration came from western and northern Europe, then in its phase of rapid population growth. Ireland, England, Scandinavia, and Germany were the leading countries of emigration. After 1880, southern and eastern Europe became the major source of immigrants. Italians, Jews from Russia and Poland, Poles, Slovaks, the Slavic peoples of central Europe and the Balkan peninsula, and Greeks crossed the ocean in great numbers. These two groups are often referred to as the old and the new immigrations.

Similar mass movements from Europe occurred on a far smaller scale to Canada, South America, Australia, New Zealand, and South Africa. Probably a total of over sixty million people left Europe in the nineteenth century and perhaps three-fourths of them have remained abroad. There were also migratory movements in other parts of the world, but they were small by comparison. China, India, and Japan have been the leading countries of emigration in Asia.

It is usually assumed that the European immigrants, with the exception of Jews and other groups escaping persecution at home, were seeking improved economic opportunities. Students of migration have distinguished between the "push" of economic hardship in the country of origin and the "pull" of economic opportunity in the country of destination. They have often differed in attributing priority to one or the other in the case of particular migratory movements, but have tended to assume that the causes of migration and the motives for migrating are adequately accounted for by a simple economic "push-pull" dichotomy. Petersen's contrast between conservative and innovating migration represents a needed refinement of the "push-pull" theory, one that takes into account the relativity of such notions as "hardship" and "opportunity" to the migrants' level of aspiration and thus permits a distinction between the personal motives and the social causes underlying migration.[12]

Migration from Europe to the Americas in the late nineteenth and early twentieth centuries assumed the proportions of a mass movement with the result that "the principal cause of emigration [was] prior emigration" and it was no longer relevant "to inquire concerning the *individual* motivations." [13] The mass emigration from Europe took place, in fact, at a time when the standard of living in most European countries was *rising* rather than falling. It thus exemplified the general sociological principle of "relative deprivation"—that people are more likely to become discontented and adopt innovating forms of behavior when their material circumstances have somewhat improved with the result that their aspirations have also risen to the point where their "reach exceeds their grasp." This was particularly true of the "new immigration" from southern and eastern Europe after 1880. "The greatest migrations of the late nineteenth and early twentieth centuries were not chiefly composed of land-hungry peasants; they were essentially a rural-urban migration, from the overcrowded farmlands of Europe to the glittering opportunities for economic advancement presumed to exist in the cities of the New World." [14]

The example suggests that the "pull" of the expanding overseas industrial economies was the main factor attracting immigrants. And the evidence indeed indicates a close association between the volume of immigration and business conditions in the United States and Canada, amounting to a fairly regular direct corre-

lation between the two. The causal relationship between
immigration and the ups and downs of the business
cycle, however, is complex: some writers have argued
that immigration caused, or at least accentuated, depression and unemployment, while others have argued
precisely the reverse.[15] Whatever the actual effects of
immigration on economic activity may have been, the
immigrants clearly came in large numbers because they
anticipated an improvement in their material circumstances. Yet mass migration overseas was largely a
movement confined to the lower classes of the European
countries of emigration; although middle-class persons
could also expect to better themselves materially by a
move to America, their greater identification with the
national community and with its culture and institutions
reduced their inclination to take such an unpatriotic
step. Thus economic considerations alone cannot account for the actual pattern of migration if we recall
that "sometimes the basic problem is not why people
migrate but rather why they do not." [16]

Mass immigration has made an almost incalculable
contribution to American society. The rival images of
the United States as a "melting pot" and as a culturally
pluralist "nation of nations" reflect the importance of
immigration in American experience.[17] The greatest
problems of acculturation were faced by the later immigrants, most of whom came from comparatively poor
and culturally and economically backward countries and
were Catholic, Jewish, or Greek Orthodox in religion,
rather than Protestant like the peoples of the old immigration with the notable exception of the Catholic
Irish. Today, forty years after the shutting off of mass
immigration, the ethnic diversity of the American population remains one of its most striking characteristics
and, in spite of successful acculturation in the majority
of cases, ethnic origin continues to exert a powerful
influence on social and political behavior.

International Migration in the Twentieth Century

We have been considering both the motives for migrating and the countries of origin of immigrants. But
the willingness of the countries of destination to receive
large numbers of immigrants from Europe was also a
necessary condition for the great migrations of the nineteenth century. By the fourth decade of the twentieth
century, all of the leading countries of immigration had
abandoned their policies of virtually unrestricted entry
and were controlling both the quantity and quality of
immigration in various ways. Quotas limiting the number of new entrants from each country or racial group,
preferences for immigrants with certain occupational
skills, stricter provisions governing the granting of citizenship, and outright bans on immigration from areas
whose inhabitants were considered unassimilable became the rule. The first laws establishing national quotas
in the United States were passed in 1922 and probably
the entire twenty-five year period after 1925 saw fewer
newcomers to the United States than the single year
1907.

Numerous reasons existed for the change in policy.
Many Americans, influenced by racist theories, began
to fear further changes in the ethnic composition of
the American population. The quota laws of the 1920's
established fixed ratios between the numbers admitted
from each country which corresponded to the ratios
between citizens of different national origins in the
population enumerated at the 1890 census, thus dis-
criminating against central and eastern European countries whose nationals constituted the bulk of immigration after 1890. Two wars with Germany and the present
conflict with the Soviet Union have given rise to fears
that new immigrants might become nuclei of nationalis-
tic or ideological subversion. In all the formerly leading

receiving countries, domestic unemployment and agricultural overproduction during the Great Depression of the 1930's led pressure groups of industrial workers and farmers to oppose any liberalization of the immigration laws. Moreover, the depression reduced the economic differential between Europe and the overseas countries with the result that while the depression lasted, return immigration to Europe often exceeded emigration. Long-run trends in the direction of increasing industrialization and declining population growth have made it easier for European countries to absorb the peasant populations which in the nineteenth century were the main source of overseas emigration.[18]

As control over immigration has become more common, so has control over emigration. The Japanese and Italian governments sponsored colonization schemes in the 1930's, and Nazi Germany and the Soviet Union virtually banned all emigration except for certain categories of "political undesirables." Political persecution, like religious persecution in previous ages, has become a leading motive for migration, although the volume of refugee immigration has been a trickle compared with the mass migrations of the previous century.

Since World War II, political and economic dislocations have encouraged a revival of overseas emigration from Europe. In the first postwar decade, 1946-1955, the net out-migration from Europe amounted to four and one-half million, the largest volume of out-migration since the United States adopted restrictive immigration laws in the 1920's.[19] The largest contributions were from the southern European countries of Italy, Spain, and Portugal, but the British Isles and Germany also made sizable contributions. The relatively small country of the Netherlands has officially encouraged emigration, particularly to Canada, since the war; the Netherlands has long been unique among western European nations in maintaining relatively high levels of fertility and population growth.[20]

Postwar European immigration has been sufficient to make sizable contributions to the population growth of such sparsely populated countries as Canada, Australia, and New Zealand. But in contrast to the nineteenth century, the governments of the receiving countries have been selective with respect to whom they will admit. The only important new source of immigration to the United States has been the island of Puerto Rico, whose inhabitants are citizens of the United States and cannot be excluded by quota laws.

Another form of controlled migration has emerged in the twentieth century, one which was common in the past but was believed to have been permanently banished from history in the half-century before World War I: the forced transfer of entire ethnic groups or whole segments of society. The most striking examples of the ruthlessly enforced migrations carried out by modern totalitarian states are the Soviet removal of *kulaks* to sites for new cities and of ethnic colonies like the Tatars and Volga Germans to labor camps during World War II, and the Nazi transportation of Jews across Europe to the death camps and of slave laborers from occupied countries to German industrial cities. The contrast with the free individual migration of the nineteenth century could not be greater. True, these examples of forced migration refer for the most part to internal rather than international movements, but it is characteristic of totalitarianism that "the totalitarian dictator rules his own country like a foreign conqueror." [21] The mass expulsion of Germans from Czechoslovakia and Poland after the war, and the exchange of populations between India and Pakistan, are other cases of the compulsory transfer of peoples. Forced and impelled migration has once again in the conflict-ridden world of the mid-twentieth century become a major source of population change.

Migration Pressures in the World Today

Accelerating population growth in the overcrowded Asian countries and increased awareness of the great disparity between their living standards and those of the West have created a tremendous pent-up migration potential. Mass migration from the Eastern areas of actual or potential population explosion to Western areas of relatively stable population has been advocated by some as a solution to the population problems of the swarming countries of Asia and North Africa.

Western nations, however, have long been unwilling to open their doors to unrestricted immigration of Asians. Chinese were first excluded from the United States as long ago as 1880. Racial prejudice, the conviction that Asian immigrants would undercut wage levels, and the not unrealistic fear that they would simply transfer their habits of high fertility and low living standards to a new locality with an adverse effect on its standard of life have been the main reasons for opposition. To be effective in alleviating population pressure, emigration from nations such as China, India, and Japan would have to be on a very large scale indeed. The reluctance of countries with small populations capable of absorbing heavy immigration to admit large numbers of racially and culturally dissimilar peoples is understandable, however selfish it may appear to humanitarians. Even Latin America, the region of the world most anxious to encourage immigration and especially that of land-hungry peasants, rigorously limits the admission of Asians.

In any case migration is no long-run solution to population pressure in high-fertility areas. "Migrations throughout the long history of Asia served to diffuse people, culture, and poverty, not to solve population problems." [22] Resentment of the exclusionist attitude of the West, however, is likely to increase as long as death rates continue to drop in the overcrowded countries, while birth rates remain high. Once again the urgency of assisting Asia to make the transition to low levels of fertility and mortality becomes apparent.

Internal Migration

Although international migrations have usually attracted greater popular and scholarly attention, the migrations of peoples within the borders of national territories have far exceeded them in volume. The right to free movement within a nation's territorial boundaries is frequently constitutionally guaranteed, regarded as inherent in the very concept of citizenship, and legitimately withheld only from minors, criminals, and the mentally ill or defective. Modern totalitarian states, however, have often restricted or abolished this right for large numbers of their citizens and have introduced contemporary equivalents of the system of "internal passports" which so often aroused resentment among the subjects of autocratic regimes of the past. With the exception of the compulsory population transfers carried out by the Nazis and Communists, internal migrations in modern countries are largely of the free individual and collectively channeled, or mass, forms. Internal movements do not differ greatly from international movements in their causation and motivation. In-migrants, however, are less likely to face acute problems of acculturation than immigrants with the result that personal, noneconomic motives play a larger part in internal than in international migrations. However, the major internal migratory movements in the modern world represent similar responses to the "pushes" and "pulls" of economic adversity and opportunity that loom so large in international migrations.

The chief form of internal migration in modern times, and probably before the modern era as well, is rural-urban migration. In 1790, 5 per cent of the

American population lived in cities and towns, while 95 per cent lived in rural areas. By 1960, 70 per cent were classified by the census as urban and only 30 per cent as rural. Between these two dates there was a steady increase in the percentage of city-dwellers. The population growth of cities has been the result of heavy in-migration from rural areas rather than of rapid natural increase. Urban birth rates have everywhere been lower than rural rates, even before the industrial and demographic revolutions in Western countries. Moreover, urban death rates were markedly higher than rural rates in the early period of the industrial revolution and are still somewhat higher in most Western nations.

Changes in patterns of land use in response to commercial considerations (the "enclosures" of British economic history), and increases in agricultural productivity due to improved farming practices have continuously reduced the manpower needs of agriculture in economically developing countries, freeing or forcing small farmers, peasants, and agricultural laborers to leave the land and move to the cities. The industrial labor force of all modernized nations has been created and augmented in this fashion, whether the dislocation experienced by the displaced rural population has been rapid and brutal, as in England in the early decades of the industrial revolution and in Russia during the 1920's and 1930's, or more gradual, with the expanding city's promise of a higher standard of living serving as an effective migratory magnet over several generations. Industrialization has, in short, everywhere been preceded by agricultural revolutions which have enabled people to leave the land and enter nonagricultural occupations. Thus, most rural-urban migration also represents a shift from agriculture to industrial and urban-centered nonmanual occupations. By 1960 slightly under a tenth of the population of the United States consisted of people living on farms, yet they managed to produce enough food to feed the remaining 90 per cent and leave huge surpluses for export. Much international migration has also been part of this world-wide rural-urban movement resulting from interdependent agricultural and industrial revolutions.

The two major migrations within the United States in the recent past have been the continuing westward movement of population and the exodus of Negroes from the South to the northern and western states. Although defined in regional terms, both these migrations have to some degree been rural-urban in character, the movement of Negroes almost entirely so. As late as 1940 the bulk of the Negro population still lived in the South and was predominantly rural, but by 1960 40 per cent of the Negroes lived outside the South and nearly two-thirds were urban residents. The effects of this population shift on race relations are far-reaching: race relations have increasingly become a national rather than a Southern regional problem. The westward movement of population has in recent decades greatly enhanced the political and economic importance of the Pacific coastal states and shows no signs of abating. While these two migrations have been outstanding in recent American history, the United States in general has become a nation of nomads, with one person out of every five moving to another house each year.

Demographic Effects of Migration

The effects of migration on population size and growth are more complex than a first glance suggests. The effects on both the country or territory of origin and of destination have to be separately considered. Obviously, the immediate effect is that the migrants reduce the population of the country they leave and increase the population of the country they enter. But their departure may alter the situation in a way that affects mortality and fertility rates, the other components of population growth, and thus may over time indirectly influence population size and growth in a contrary direction. By alleviating population pressure, emigration may both lower mortality rates and encourage earlier marriage and more frequent childbearing with the result that the loss of the emigrants is eventually more than compensated. Similarly, immigration may have a "multiplier effect" on population growth in the country of destination if the immigrants come from an area with higher fertility rates than their new homeland. They add not merely themselves but their future progeny to the population. To some extent all migration has such an effect on the population of the country of destination, because migrants are nearly always youthful and thus alter the age structure of the population in a direction favorable to higher fertility and lower mortality. Exceptions are refugee migrations, which tend to be less selective of the young, and migrations to frontier regions, which largely involve males alone.

It has sometimes been maintained, however, that immigration (or in-migration) does not increase the population of the receiving area in the long run, because it causes the original inhabitants either to lower their birth rates or to emigrate themselves.[23] Successive waves of immigrants entered American society at the bottom of the class structure and by taking over the low-paying and less skilled jobs permitted the native-born to move upwards on the occupational scale. Since class or occupational position tends to be inversely correlated with fertility in countries undergoing economic development, immigration may have hastened the decline in the birth rate of the native-born population by enabling them to improve their social status more rapidly.

Nevertheless, it is doubtful that this loss of births resulting from immigration has been sufficient to compensate for the addition to the population of the immigrants themselves and the gain in births following from the habits of high fertility which they brought with them from their peasant societies of origin. Warren S. Thompson has concluded:

> It is the author's judgement that, although the influx of great numbers of immigrants may have hastened the decline of the native birth rate, it has also so added materially to our growth, that our population is larger now than it would have been had there been no immigration since 1800.[24]

There has been less disagreement among population students on the effects of emigration on the population of the country of origin. In countries where fertility is not under voluntary control, emigration probably does not appreciably reduce population growth unless it is on a very large scale. In countries where populations live close to the subsistence level, emigration may lower death rates by temporarily alleviating population pressure and may thus promote a greater natural increase that more than compensates for the loss of the emigrants and their prospective progeny. However, where people have learned to control fertility in order to benefit from a higher standard of living and the birth rate has become the main variable determining the rate of natural increase, emigration may result in net losses of numbers and relieve economic distress arising out of population pressure.

After the great potato famine, Ireland succeeded in reducing her numbers from about eight to four millions by combining fertility control (largely by postponed marriage) with mass emigration overseas. Emigration cannot be considered a solution to population pressure *unless* fertility control is practiced by the country of emigration so that the lower mortality following short-run alleviation of pressure is offset by low fertility. Fertility in underdeveloped countries such as India and China is at the present time unrestricted, so emigration is unlikely to solve their population problem, quite apart from the unreadiness of the West to accept mass immigration from Asia.

People and Resources: The Malthusian Problem

Malthus' Principle of Population

Thomas Robert Malthus, an early nineteenth-century economist, is generally considered to be the father of population study as a field of scholarship. Since the publication in 1798 of the first edition of his *An Essay on the Principle of Population,* his views have been the subject of heated controversy. Few students of population today accept his theory of population in the form in which it was originally stated, yet many modern writers advance views which may, without doing them undue violence, be described as neo-Malthusian. There have been able theorists on population before and after Malthus, but he alone succeeded in making his name almost synonymous with the field of population study, at least among those who are not professional population specialists. "His true claim to fame," James A. Field observes, "rests not on the originality of his ideas but rather on the fact that people listened to what he said." [1]

In essence, Malthus' theory was that human populations tend to increase at a more rapid rate than the food supply needed to sustain them. Malthus based this conclusion on several postulates about man's material needs, sexual instincts, and reproductive capacities. He believed that sexual passion was a powerful, virtually uncontrollable, and unchanging component of human nature. Thus gratification of sexual desires carries with it the risk of producing children for whom the means of support are unavailable. Man's biological need for food and his sexual impulses are inescapably in conflict.

Malthus' principle of population can best be stated in his own words. In the second edition of his famous *Essay* he reduced it to three propositions:

> 1. Population is necessarily limited by the means of subsistence. 2. Population invariably increases where the means of subsistence increase, unless prevented by some very powerful and obvious checks. 3. These checks, and the checks which repress the superior power of population, and keep its effects on a level with the means of subsistence, are all resolvable into moral restraint, vice, and misery.[2]

Malthus believed that he had discovered an impregnable argument against the optimistic views of social progress advanced by William Godwin and other liberal reformers of the eighteenth century. If population always increases to the point where any further increase is checked by the limits of the food supply, obviously material progress can produce no lasting improvement in the living conditions of mankind. Instead of permitting the existing population to lead a more comfortable life, increases in food production will merely allow a larger population to subsist at the same low levels that prevailed before the rise in food output. Thus, Malthus asserted, the hopes of the Godwinian believers in progress were vain; they defied the "natural law" of population growth.

The checks imposed on population growth by the means of subsistence were, Malthus held in his third proposition, all "resolvable into moral restraint, vice, and misery." Those conditions which produce vice and misery he called *positive checks;* moral restraint he labeled the *preventive check.* Wars, infanticide, plagues, and famine constitute the major positive checks; some of these, like plagues and famines, "appear to arise unavoidably from the laws of nature and may be called exclusively misery." Others, such as wars and infanticide, "we obviously bring upon ourselves," but "they are brought upon us by vice, and their consequences are misery." [3] By moral restraint, the sole preventive check to population increase Malthus recognized, he meant the prudential postponement of marriage for the purpose of avoiding reproduction when the individual is unable to support children.

The positive checks, in short, are those which limit population growth by raising the death rate, while the preventive check achieves the same effect by lowering the birth rate. Clearly there are other means of lowering the birth rate than postponing marriage, notably voluntary birth control, which has in fact been the means chiefly responsible for reducing fertility in Western countries. But Malthus refused to countenance birth control and classed it with vice. "A promiscuous intercourse to such a degree as to prevent the birth of children," he wrote, "seems to lower, in the most marked manner, the dignity of human nature." [4] Malthus' disapproval of birth control stemmed less from moral objections to sexual pleasure freed from procreative aims than from his conviction that man was naturally indolent and needed the fear of inability to support his children to goad him into efforts to improve his economic situation; if sexual gratification could be achieved without the risk of conception, human progress, Malthus thought, would come to a standstill.[5]

Thus the postponement of marriage until a man is able to support a wife and at least six children, in conjunction with total premarital sexual abstinence, was the only preventive check Malthus admitted and dignified with the name moral restraint. Since he doubted the capacity of mankind, in particular the lower classes, to exercise this restraint, he was inclined to believe that human society would always be threatened by the positive checks of starvation, disease, and war. In his later years he became more hopeful, but his fundamental pessimism earned for economics the title of "the dismal science."

Major Criticisms of Malthus

The first and purely logical objection to Malthus' principle is the ambiguity with which it is often stated. Malthus spoke of population as having a constant *tendency to increase* at a rate faster than the means of subsistence. Sometimes it is unclear whether he meant that population *does in fact* increase more rapidly than the means of subsistence or merely that it *could do so if not checked*. Except for short periods in societies where the average standard of life is well above the minimum subsistence level, the former is clearly an impossibility. As Kingsley Davis argues:

> The very fact that numbers are increasing indicates that the means to support them is increasing too. Otherwise mortality would have risen and the population would never have grown to its present size. To think of the world's population as "outrunning" its normal food supply is like thinking of the hind feet of a horse outrunning its front feet.[6]

At times Malthus so qualified his law that he appeared to be claiming merely that population has the *capacity* to increase more rapidly than food production. This is undeniable, but it leaves entirely open the question of the degree to which at a given time the capacity is actually being realized. As Ian Bowen has pointed out, the principle is irrefutable when stated in this way, for whenever a case is found in which the means of subsistence are abundant and population growth falls short of Malthus' maximum rate, *by definition* the checks are at work preventing a more rapid increase.[7]

There are also empirical objections to Malthus' law. His gloomy insistence on the ever-present pressure of numbers on subsistence has scarcely been justified by

the history of the Western world since his day. He
had the misfortune—from the standpoint of the plau-
sibility of his theory—of writing on the eve of the industrial revolution in England and of the opening up to
cultivation of the grassy plains of North America. The
resulting increase in wealth was attended by rapid population growth, which, in contrast to expectations
derived from the Malthusian theory, failed to prevent
the occurrence of a general rise in the standard of living that has continued almost unabated to the present
day.

As Malthus himself conceded in later versions of his
theory, he had underestimated the extent to which
what he called fresh starts in agriculture might enable
the means of subsistence to increase more rapidly than
population, for at least limited periods of time. Yet
the technological revolution in agriculture still continuing today has made it possible "to grow two blades
of grass when only one grew before" on a scale never
imagined by Malthus. He tended to identify the limits
of food production with the limits of cultivable land
area and minimized the possibility of great improvements in agricultural technique. Nor did he foresee the
extent to which England would be able to support a
growing population on food imports from sparsely
settled areas overseas.

Nevertheless, the great increases in agricultural productivity of the past century and a half may have
simply temporarily defeated Malthus' law, although they
clearly invalidate his oft-expressed view that there
was a *constant* short-run pressure of numbers on resources. The decline of the birth rate is a more serious
empirical contradiction of his theory. As we have
seen, the practice of birth control after marriage,
largely by means of contraceptive techniques, has been
responsible for the decline in fertility that has checked
Western population growth. Only one Western nation,
Catholic Ireland, has followed Malthus' advice and

controlled fertility primarily by marrying late rather than by practicing birth control after marriage. Considering Malthus' disapproval of birth control, it is ironic that his name is almost inseparably linked in the popular mind with the birth control movement. The early propagandists for birth control used Malthusian arguments, and to this day proponents of birth control have called themselves neo-Malthusians, the "neo" symbolizing their recognition that Malthus himself did not approve of birth control as a preventive check to population growth.

Clearly Westerners have not elected to limit the size of their families in order to prevent an otherwise inevitable operation of the eliminative checks of starvation and disease. Unless Malthus' term "means of subsistence" is taken to mean not only the sheer minimum necessary for physical survival but also all of the diverse and culturally variable material wants of modern populations, it cannot be concluded that limited means of subsistence have been the chief factor preventing fertility from realizing its maximum biological potential. The desire for a high standard of living which has arisen in advanced urban-industrial societies underlies the trend towards smaller families.

Actually, it is one of Malthus' inconsistencies that he often recognized this himself, observing that "a decided taste for the conveniences and comforts of life" does not "operate as an encouragement to early marriages" but often has the reverse effect.[8] One would expect, therefore, that as more and more people were raised above subsistence level, their desire to maintain their "conveniences and comforts" would encourage them to avoid excessive childbearing. And this is precisely what has happened in industrial societies, although the means of avoiding childbearing has been birth control rather than the postponement of marriage favored by Malthus.

Although the Malthusian law no longer threatens

Western societies, many people maintain that it still applies to overcrowded, underdeveloped countries such as India and China, and that it was applicable to most human societies before the modern era. If by the Malthusian law one means simply the pressure of numbers on resources, this is indisputably true. Malthus' great contribution to social thought was to call attention to population pressure as a major source of human suffering. Yet Malthus' view of human nature was that of a biological determinist. Even in overcrowded societies living close to the bare subsistence level there are, as we saw in Chapter 4, social and cultural restrictions on fertility unrelated to population pressure. Conceding the rigor of Malthus' thought, the correctness of his insistence that human numbers cannot go on increasing indefinitely, and the relevance of population pressure to the social and economic plight of contemporary underdeveloped nations, the conception of an unchanging, biologically fixed human nature from which he derived his law has long since been rejected by social scientists.

The Contemporary Population Debate

Since World II there has been a resurgence of fear that world population is increasing at a rate which threatens low-income areas with mass famine and malnutrition, and high-income areas with a reduction of living standards. The increased responsibilities of the United States as a world power have forced Americans to become more aware of the problems of poverty-stricken and overcrowded parts of the world. This awareness and the postwar rise of the birth rate in Western nations themselves have led to renewed concern with the world population-food ratio, in contrast to the 1930's when the possible dangers of underpopulation were more widely publicized.

But it is not merely professional population students who have become concerned over the rapid increase in world population. The world problems created by population growth have become a matter of public debate as well. Students of population who have long been concerned with the relation between the increase of numbers and the availability of resources to support them, find their subject at last receiving the attention its importance merits. Public discussion is unquestionably preferable to indifference, but it must be admitted that many current pronouncements on the "population explosion" reveal more about the passions and doctrinal beliefs of the speaker than about the realities of the problem. Not doubt this is inevitable where moral and religious convictions regarding the family, sex, childbearing, the role of women, and the responsibilities of the rich towards the poor—always emotion-laden topics —are at the very heart of the matter. "Population studies," as one writer has observed, "are basically concerned with primitive instincts—so primitive, so remote and fierce, and yet so near to consciousness, that the objectivity of any human . . . observer must always be in doubt unless he is content to describe facts." [9]

The facts of world population growth and the distribution of world resources are not subject to controversy. The desirability of the attainment of a higher standard of living by the overcrowded, underdeveloped countries by means that avoid war or the risk of war is also generally acknowledged. Disagreement centers on rival interpretations of the facts, interpretations which clash on the questions of whether population growth is an aid or an obstacle to economic development and on what the effects of limiting growth by encouraging the spread of birth control are likely to be. These differences are usually rooted in political ideologies or in religious convictions concerning the morality of various methods of birth control. Both official Communist doctrine and the Catholic church have, for different reasons, adopted positions that can loosely be characterized **as** "anti-Malthusian" in the sense that they deny the relevance of population pressure to the economic and social problems of the underdeveloped countries and oppose governmental efforts to reduce the rate of population growth in these countries by encouraging the spread of family limitation by contraceptive means.[10]

On the other hand, the neo-Malthusian writers call attention to the fact that birth rates remain high in many parts of the world, death rates are falling rapidly, few new lands open to settlement remain, and the exploitive use of land already under cultivation has reduced its productivity and led to widespread erosion of valuable topsoil.[11] The neo-Malthusians paint horrendous pictures of a future world in which, if present population growth rates continue, people will be packed together shoulder to shoulder covering every square foot of space on earth. The inference is drawn, or at least suggested, that unless the present rate of increase falls we are likely to end up living in such a sardine-can world.

Too often the whole subject is discussed as if only two points of view in direct conflict with one another existed: that of those who wish to limit population growth by means of birth control on the one hand, and that of those who favor an all-out effort to raise food production on the other. Yet most professional students of the problem refuse to see these as mutually exclusive alternatives and advocate a joint program of encouraging both birth control and economic development. Moreover, they favor an economic development plan that is designed to increase the production of all goods and services rather than merely of food alone. The governments of several underdeveloped countries, most notably India, are already committed to promoting the voluntary practice of birth control as part of the general objective of modernizing their economies and raising the standard of living.

Since what we loosely call the standard of living of a country is determined by the relation between the size of its population and its total economic output, it makes obvious sense, if we wish to raise that standard, to try to influence both sides of the numbers-output equation. More accurately, it makes sense to try to control population growth as well as to increase output *if* the population is already so large and so dense that additional people will have no room to spread out onto unsettled land and *if* additions to the population will not increase the productivity of labor by making possible greater occupational specialization. These conditions are clearly present in India, Pakistan, China, and Egypt, and they are just as clearly absent in Canada, Australia, and the larger South American countries. Thus the high rates of growth in the latter nations provide little cause for anxiety, while the somewhat lower growth rates of the former are a major cause of concern.

The opponents of the neo-Malthusians, who might be called neo-Godwinians, are likely to counter alarmism over the world population explosion with glowing estimates of the purely technical possibilities of increasing world agricultural output.[12] They point to new lands in the tropics which might be brought into production, to the higher yields obtainable by using improved farming methods in underdeveloped countries, to economic reorganizations that promise to increase productivity, and to unrealized possibilities of growing food plants in water tanks, farming the ocean floor, and synthesizing foodstuffs from wood and even from inorganic materials. If all, or even some, of these things were done, they insist, the earth could support a far larger population than at present. And there remains the prospect of space travel to alleviate the continued pressure of growing numbers by permitting emigration to other planets, so the sky is literally no limit.[13]

While these contentions are undeniably true, the fact that the obstacles to creating a "world economy of abundance" are political, economic, and social, that is, rooted in social institutions and belief systems created

by man, does not make the problem of balancing population and resources any easier to solve. It is a mistake
to equate what is *technically* possible with what has a
reasonable probability of happening in a world of com-
peting national sovereignties, wars, revolutions, and
ideological and racial antagonisms.[14] The herculean
effort required to maintain a rate of economic growth
high enough to keep perpetually ahead of uncontrolled
population growth is just not likely to be forthcoming.
Social institutions and attitudes have their own inertia
and intractability to change, which often prove to be as
formidable obstacles to increasing economic production
as biological and geographic barriers. Moreover, glowing estimates of future advances in productivity usually
concentrate on possible gains in food production, ignor-
ing the fact that human beings, however well-fed, also
need *space*. Never-ending population growth would
ultimately lead to a shortage of space even if the problem of food supply were solved.

The advocates of birth control as a check to population growth believe on good evidence that reduced
growth will make possible more rapid economic progress
to eliminate the terrible poverty afflicting the majority
of the inhabitants of the world's underdeveloped countries.[15] They fear that without a slowing up of population increase these countries may simply end up supporting more people at the same low standard of living,
whereas a successful program combining fertility control with economic development would enable a smaller
total population to achieve what we in the West consider to be minimum standards for human decency and
dignity. The accusation often made that the proponents
of birth control are misanthropes who want fewer people in the world and lack faith in the ability of science
and technology to raise the standard of living is, therefore, absurd.

Sometimes, it is true, those who voice alarm over
world population growth resort to scare statistics which

obscure the real reasons for alarm. The point about the imaginary sardine-can world they describe is not that such a world is a real and unpleasant possibility, but rather that it is inconceivable. Long before we were confined to standing room only on the earth's surface, population growth would fall as a result of a rise in mortality. The population *cannot* go on increasing indefinitely; it *must* eventually reach a point of stability. This is the core of truth in Malthus' often contradictory formulations and it is evaded with amazing persistence by the neo-Godwinians who do not wish to face up to the eventual necessity of population control. While it is possible for the world to support a population a good deal larger than the present one, the fundamental choice we face is between achieving population stability by lowering the birth rate as opposed to achieving it by allowing the death rate to rise. Those who object to birth control ought to be prepared to declare themselves in favor of higher mortality instead. The world's present population problems could be solved for a long time by a few mass famines, a world-wide repetition of the Great Plagues of medieval Europe, or, for that matter, by several well-placed thermonuclear bombs. Are we prepared to see them solved in this way?

But it is by no means certain that mass genocide, demographically motivated wars, or even the milder policy of holding back death control measures could finally "solve" the population problem. A temporary rise in mortality might facilitate rapid economic development, which would then lead to the adoption of family planning. But more probably, the result would be a cycle of wars, civil strife, mass bitterness and apathy that would themselves retard or prevent economic development. It is sometimes argued that the Black Death, which carried away from one-third to one-half of the population of Europe in the 14th century, was a necessary condition for the later occurrence of the Industrial Revolution. But here again we are probably dealing with a confusion between short- and long-run considerations. Even though the Black Death was not a man-made disaster, two centuries of disorder, violence, and cultural lag intervened between its ravages and the immense releases of human energy we call the Renaissance and the Reformation. And most historians agree that the troubles of this period, "the waning of the Middle Ages," stemmed directly from the trauma of mass death by plague and famine. Would man-made holocausts have a lesser effect?

In the first round of debate on the issue of population and food supply in modern Western history, William Godwin answered Thomas Robert Malthus with the prediction that the day would come when mankind would be able to grow its entire food supply in a single flowerpot. Godwin may prove to be ultimately right; he was clearly right in stressing the inventiveness and creativity of human beings as against Malthus' insistence on ineluctable, unchanging laws of nature. And certainly the hysterical insistence of some contemporary neo-Malthusians that science not only is incapable of saving us but even aggravates our problems is not convincing,[16] nor is their contention that although Westerners have achieved a state of demographic grace by adopting birth control, the peoples of Asia and Africa are incapable of learning from their experience. Let us assume, however, that the marvels of science and technology do succeed in creating a world in which productivity rises at unprecedented rates. Those who talk blithely of algae out of the sea and rockets to Mars rarely pause to ask themselves whether we really want to live in a world where population pressure compels us to rely on such expedients, leaving us no choice. Even if other planets are habitable, astronomers doubt whether they would be very pleasant places to live. And even though a sardine-can world is a fantasy and a larger world population can in principle be comfortably supported, are we utterly indifferent to considerations of space and density? Do we care nothing if the world resembles a rabbit warren so long as people get enough to eat? [17] It is curious that those who oppose the universal adoption of birth control should so often think of themselves as conservatives, as upholders of tradition, for the transformation of our way of life required to support a vastly larger population would be far greater than that resulting from the world-wide practice of birth control.

We need have no difficulty in imagining what a world in which birth control is universally practiced would be like. For, as we have seen in Chapters 4 and 5, birth control is *already* widely practiced in the major countries of Western civilization. The belief that the mass use of contraceptive birth control is an untried, new-fangled notion amounting to an unprecedented departure from the wisdom and restraint of the past is without rational foundation. The West has already rejected uncontrolled human fertility with the result that her population growth is able flexibly to adjust itself to changing economic and social trends. This is the goal the developing nations of the "Third World" must now achieve under far more difficult conditions. It will undoubtedly be difficult to persuade tradition-minded peasants in underdeveloped areas to adopt effective methods of birth control—even if a new, simpler method such as a pill is invented in time—before they have experienced the social and economic transformations that created the desire for small families in the West. But the chances of doing so are far better than the chances of winning a never-ending race between economic growth and population increase.

Those who do not approve of birth control would do better to base their opposition on religious or absolutist moral grounds alone. These are, of course, the real grounds for opposition in most cases, but their upholders invariably seek additional support by advancing questionable arguments about the purely secular problem of the relation between population growth and economic progress. Even those who do not share it can respect the integrity of a genuine religious position, if not the dogmatism of an erroneous social and economic theory such as Communist anti-Malthusianism. But instead of hiding behind shaky arguments, such a position should be stated forthrightly even when it can only make the ancient demand, unacceptable to many of us, that justice be done though the world perish.

Population and Economic Development

Whatever measures of economic well-being one selects, the contrast between the nations of Western civilization and the rest of the world, containing over half of the earth's total population, stands out.[18] The non-Western countries are poorer in per capita income, their per capita food consumption is lower and nutritionally less adequate,[19] their agriculture is less productive, and their social institutions encourage high fertility which in combination with declining mortality makes possible explosive population growth threatening to intensify the pressure of population on resources and condemn ever-increasing numbers of people to poverty and malnutrition. Kingsley Davis has ably described the vicious circle in which the Indian peasant is caught, a description that is applicable to peasant cultivators in other densely populated Asian countries.[20] The peasant must devote all his efforts to wresting a meager subsistence from his small plot of ground; his poverty is so great that he cannot afford to apply capital such as machine-made implements or commercial fertilizers to his land in order to increase its productivity and check the ravages of erosion and declining soil fertility. To obtain the maximum yield from it he can only apply manpower, so he is motivated to raise large families, thus creating more mouths to be fed from the land's limited produce. He is constantly in the position of trying to raise himself by his own bootstraps to break out of this vicious circle. Nor can the pile-up of people on the land be alleviated by migration to cities so long as capital investment in transportation and manufacturing is lagging. The continuation of rapid population increase perpetuates this lag by requiring the constant diversion of capital and manpower to agriculture in order to increase the food supply in circumstances where there is little room for expansion of crop acreage.[21]

If we assume that industrialization would, as it has in the Western world, "automatically" create the social conditions favoring smaller families and thus of itself cut back the rate of population growth, we need to remind ourselves that it was in the early stages of industrialization that the greatest population increases took place in the West. And the underdeveloped Asian countries with few exceptions already have far larger and denser populations than western Europe at the beginning of the industrial revolution. The same is true of several Latin-American countries, although, in common with Africa south of the Sahara, the larger continental South American countries are relatively thinly populated and can more readily support additional numbers than can underdeveloped Asia and North Africa. In the larger countries of the latter group, India, China, and Indonesia, even a low rate of natural increase adds colossal absolute numbers to a base population already pressing heavily on resources.

Economic development cannot, therefore, be undertaken in the densely settled underdeveloped areas without considering how it will affect and be affected by demographic trends. In contrast to the past experience of the West and the possible future experience of Africa and South America,[22] Asia cannot await the automatic transition to low fertility that has invariably followed industrialization elsewhere. A population policy designed to reduce fertility must be an integral part of development schemes if the gains of higher productivity are not to be used merely to support a larger population whose further growth will eventually wipe out the very achievements in mortality control and improved living conditions that have already been won. The government of India has realized this and become the second nation to adopt an official anti-natalist policy of encouraging birth control (Japan was the first), and even the doctrinally anti-Malthusian government of Communist China has given uncertain signs of recognizing it.[23]

Some means of fertility control have seemed almost as offensive to Western sensibilities as would a policy of deliberately increasing the death rate. Western social scientists and medical specialists have generally favored the voluntary use of chemical or mechanical contraceptives by individual married couples. But it is beginning to appear that sterilization and abortion may have greater appeal to some peoples as forms of birth control than the advanced techniques favored by Western advisors.[24] Nor is it clear that an improved oral contraceptive or the new intra-uterine devices that have recently loomed large in discussions of population control would necessarily have greater appeal. Since the goal of anti-natalist policies in the underdeveloped world must be to achieve fertility decline *before* rather than after the achievement of full social and economic modernization, it ill behooves Westerners to frown on the encouragement of methods like sterilization and abortion. The underdeveloped countries simply cannot afford to delay fertility reduction until after they have attained the benefits of modernization, and perhaps contraceptive birth control will itself have to be viewed as one of those benefits.

The gap between the economic have and have-not nations has been widening since World War II. The dangers this poses for international peace should be apparent. Even in the absence of the cold war between the Communist and Western blocs of nations, population pressure might eventually induce the larger Asian countries to invade their more thinly settled neighbors in search of additional resources.[25] The attractions of Communist totalitarianism as a drastic short-cut to economic modernization and national power may very well increase, although, as G. L. Arnold and others have argued, its appeal is likely to be greatest not to the peasant masses but to military, bureaucratic, and intellectual elites whose aspirations are blocked by traditional social structures and attitudes.[26] For these reasons the political and economic transformation of the non-Western world, a transformation that will be profoundly affected by their demographic situation, is the central issue of contemporary history.

Notes

CHAPTER 1

1 Kingsley Davis, "The Sociology of Demographic Behavior," in Robert K. Merton, Leonard Broom, and Leonard S. Cottrell, Jr. (eds.), *Sociology Today,* New York: Basic Books, 1959, p. 313.

2 See the definition of demography advanced by Hauser and Duncan in Philip M. Hauser and Otis Dudley Duncan (eds.), *The Study of Population: An Inventory and Appraisal,* Chicago: University of Chicago Press, 1959, p. 2.

3 It is fully developed by Hauser and Duncan, *op. cit.,* pp. 33–37.

4 *Ibid.,* p. 3.

5 Kingsley Davis, *Human Society,* New York: Macmillan Company, 1949, p. 552.

6 Hauser and Duncan, *op. cit.,* pp. 107–108.

7 Davis, "The Sociology of Demographic Behavior," p. 312.

8 Davis, *Human Society,* p. 551.

CHAPTER 2

1 V. Gordon Childe, *Man Makes Himself,* New York: Mentor Books, 1951, and *What Happened in History,* Harmondsworth, Middlesex: Penguin Books, rev. ed., 1954.

2 Unlike the first revolution, which is identified with the discovery of agriculture, Childe's second great revolution is not linked to a single basic invention. However, he mentions fifteen distinct inventions or improvements in earlier techniques that he sees as prerequisites for large urban concentrations of population. See *Man Makes Himself,* p. 180.

3 *Ibid.,* p. 19.

4 A. M. Carr-Saunders, *World Population,* Oxford: The Clarendon Press, 1936, p. 42; Walter F. Willcox, *Studies in American Demography,* Ithaca, N.Y.: Cornell University Press, 1940, p. 45.

5 John D. Durand, "The Population Statistics of China A.D. 2–1953," *Population Studies,* 13: 209–256 (March 1960).

6 Carr-Saunders, *op. cit.,* pp. 34–35; Willcox, *op. cit.,* pp. 47–48.

7 M. K. Bennett, *The World's Food,* New York: Harper and Brothers, 1954, pp. 16–17.

8 Carr-Saunders, *op. cit.,* p. 34.

9 One of the earliest examples of such a classification may be found in Warren S. Thompson, "Population," *American Journal of Sociology,* 34: 959–975 (May 1929). For later classifications, see Frank W. Notestein, "Population—The Long View," in Theodore W. Schultz (ed.), *Food for the World,* Chicago: University of Chicago Press, 1944, pp. 31–57; and Warren S. Thompson, "The Growth of Population," *Scientific American,* 182: 11–15 (Feb. 1950).

10 United Nations, Population Division, "The Past and Future Population of the World and Its Continents," in Joseph J. Spengler and Otis Dudley Duncan (eds.), *Demographic Analysis: Selected Readings,* Glencoe, Ill.: The Free Press, 1956, pp. 26–33.

11 The relatively low density figure shown for China in Table 2 is misleading in view of the large uninhabitable desert and mountain regions in that country.

12 Rupert Vance has claimed genuine theoretical status for the conception of the demographic transition in "Is Theory for Demographers?" *Social Forces,* 31: 9–13 (Oct. 1952).

13 See, for example, Philip M. Hauser and Otis Dudley Duncan (eds.), *The Study of Population: An Inventory and Appraisal,* Chicago: University of Chicago Press, 1959, pp. 93–96; Kingsley Davis, "The Controversial Future of the Underdeveloped Areas," in Paul K. Hatt (ed.), *World Population and Future Resources,* New York: American Book Company, 1952, pp. 22–24; Irene B. Taeuber, "The Future of Transitional Areas," in Hatt, *op. cit.,* pp. 25–38; Leighton van Nort, "On Values in Population Theory," *The Milbank Memorial Fund Quarterly,* 38: 387–395 (Oct. 1960); and "Some Issues for Transition Theory," paper, annual meet-

ings of the Population Association of America, Washington, D.C., May 1960; William Petersen, *Population,* New York: Macmillan Company, 1961, pp. 11–14.

14 Robert Gutman, "In Defense of Population Theory," *American Sociological Review,* 25: 332 (June 1960).

15 H. J. Habbakuk, "The Economic History of Modern Britain," *Journal of Economic History,* 18: 486–501 (Dec. 1958); John T. Krause, "Some Implications of Recent Works in Historical Demography," *Comparative Studies in Society and History,* 1: 164–188 (Jan. 1959); and "Some Neglected Factors in the English Industrial Revolution," *Journal of Economic History,* 19: 528–540 (Dec. 1959). For a good summary of population during the Industrial Revolution, see Petersen, *op. cit.,* pp. 376–404.

16 Kingsley Davis, "Institutional Factors Favoring High Fertility in Underdeveloped Areas," *Eugenics Quarterly,* 2: 33–39 (March 1955).

17 Bert F. Hoselitz, "Population Pressure, Industrialization and Social Mobility," *Population Studies,* 11: 123–135 (Nov. 1957).

18 Krause argues to this effect in the articles previously cited, but to the present writer his conclusions seem to go far beyond the evidence.

19 Kingsley Davis, "Fertility Control and the Demographic Transition in India," in Milbank Memorial Fund, *The Interrelations of Demographic, Economic, and Social Problems in Selected Underdeveloped Areas,* New York: Milbank Fund, 1954, pp. 66–89; Kurt B. Mayer, "Fertility Changes and Population Forecasts in the United States," *Social Research,* 26: 353–354 (Autumn 1959); William Petersen, "The Demographic Transition in the Netherlands," *American Sociological Review,* 25: 334–347 (June 1960); Irene B. Taeuber, "Japan's Demographic Transition Re-examined," *Population Studies,* 14: 28–39 (July 1960). Lorimer compares in detail the differences in the trend of fertility in nineteenth-century England and France in Frank Lorimer and others, *Culture and Human Fertility,* Paris: Unesco, 1954, pp. 206–217.

20 George J. Stolnitz, "Comparison Between Some Recent Mortality Trends in Underdeveloped Areas and Historical Trends in the West," in Milbank Memorial Fund, *Trends and Differentials in Mortality,* New York: Milbank Fund,

1956, pp. 26–34; Kingsley Davis, "The Amazing Decline of Mortality in Underdeveloped Areas," *American Economic Review*, 46: 305–318 (May 1956).

21 See Wilbert E. Moore, "Sociology and Demography," in Hauser and Duncan, *op. cit.,* p. 844.

22 Van Nort, "On Values in Population Theory," *op. cit.,* pp. 391–392.

23 Hannah Arendt, *The Origins of Totalitarianism,* New York: Harcourt, Brace & Co., 1951, pp. 304–305.

CHAPTER 3

1 The best general sociological analysis of universal individual and societal attitudes towards mortality and morbidity is Kingsley Davis, *Human Society,* New York: Macmillan Company, 1949, pp. 562–568.

2 Émile Durkheim, *Suicide,* Glencoe, Ill.: The Free Press, 1951, esp. Book Two.

3 Leighton van Nort, "On Values and Population Theory," *The Milbank Memorial Fund Quarterly,* 38: 391–392 (Oct. 1960).

4 The criminal law in Western countries, and its roots in traditional theological and moral codes, as it bears on issues pertaining to the creation and preservation of human life are reviewed critically by Glanville Williams, *The Sanctity of Life and the Criminal Law,* New York: Alfred A. Knopf, 1957.

5 John Dewey, *Human Nature and Conduct,* New York: Modern Library, 1930, pp. 135–136.

6 Davis, *op. cit.,* pp. 561–564.

7 George J. Stolnitz, "Comparison Between Some Recent Mortality Trends in Underdeveloped Areas and Historical Trends in the West," in Milbank Memorial Fund, *Trends and Differentials in Mortality,* New York: Milbank Fund, 1956, p. 34.

8 W. S. Woytinsky and E. S. Woytinsky, *World Population and Production: Trends and Outlook,* New York: Twentieth Century Fund, 1953, p. 166.

9 George C. Whipple, quoted in T. Lynn Smith, *Fundamentals of Population Study,* New York: J. B. Lippincott, 1960, p. 352.

10 Woytinsky and Woytinsky, *op. cit.*, p. 169.

11 George J. Stolnitz advances this suggestion after a comparative international survey of trends and differences in the mortality of the sexes, "A Century of International Mortality Trends: II," *Population Studies*, 10: 31 (July 1956).

12 Louis I. Dublin, Alfred J. Lotka, and Mortimer Spiegelman, *Length of Life*, New York: Ronald Press, 1949, pp. 129–131.

13 Frederick Osborn, *Preface to Eugenics*, New York: Harper and Brothers, 1951, Preface, p. xi.

14 Dublin, Lotka, and Spiegelman, *op. cit.*, pp. 165–166.

15 Adapted from United Nations, *Demographic Yearbook*, 1965, New York: United Nations, 1966, p. 767.

16 Adapted from *ibid.*

17 George J. Stolnitz, "A Century of International Mortality Trends: I," *Population Studies*, 9:53 (July 1955).

18 Kingsley Davis, "The Amazing Decline of Mortality in Underdeveloped Areas," *American Economic Review*, 46: 307–308 (May 1956).

19 Quoted by Karl F. Helleiner, "The Vital Revolution Reconsidered," *Canadian Journal of Economics and Political Science*, 23: 6 (Feb. 1957).

CHAPTER 4

1 Kingsley Davis and Judith Blake, "Social Structure and Fertility: An Analytic Framework," *Economic Development and Cultural Change*, 4: 211–235 (April 1956).

2 Kingsley Davis, *Human Society*, New York: Macmillan Company, 1949, pp. 558–559.

3 *Ibid.*, pp. 399–401.

4 Sigmund Freud, *Civilization and Its Discontents*, New York: Doubleday Anchor Books, 1958; Herbert Marcuse, *Eros and Civilization*, Boston: Beacon Press, 1955.

5 A possible exception may be the Australian aborigine practice of subincision performed on the male sexual organ. Opinions differ both as to whether it actually reduces fecundity and whether it is intended to do so or possesses merely ritual significance.

6 Davis and Blake, *op. cit.*, p. 213.

7 Royal Commission on Population, *Report,* London: His Majesty's Stationery Office, 1949, pp. 24–25.

8 *Ibid.,* Table XVI, p. 25.

9 *Ibid.,* p. 26.

10 Joseph J. Spengler lists the huge variety of causes that have been invoked to explain the long decline of fertility in France in *France Faces Depopulation,* Durham, N.C.: Duke University Press, 1938, Chap. 7.

11 Royal Commission on Population, *op. cit.,* p. 32.

12 D. E. C. Eversely, *Social Theories of Fertility and the Malthusian Debate,* Oxford: The Clarendon Press, 1959, especially pp. 254–260.

13 For evidence on the use of *coitus interruptus* and rhythm, as well as the more efficient appliance methods of contraception, in the United States and Britain, see Pascal K. Whelpton, Arthur A. Campbell, and John E. Patterson, *Fertility and Family Planning in the United States,* Princeton: Princeton University Press, 1966, pp. 278–279.

14 The difference between these measures, and their interrelation, is discussed in detail by Norman B. Ryder, "The Structure and Tempo of Current Fertility," in National Bureau of Economic Research, *Demographic and Economic Change in Developed Countries,* Princeton: Princeton University Press, 1960, pp. 117–131.

15 Ansley J. Coale, "Comments," in *ibid.,* p. 135.

16 Pascal K. Whelpton has shown in detail that this was true at least up to 1954 for the United States. Wilson H. Grabill, Clyde V. Kiser, and Pascal K. Whelpton, *The Fertility of American Women,* New York: John Wiley and Sons, 1958, pp. 365–371.

17 Halvor Gille, "An International Survey of Recent Fertility Trends," in National Bureau of Economic Research, *op. cit.,* pp. 17–34.

18 Norman B. Ryder and Charles F. Westoff, "The Use of Oral Contraception in the U.S., 1965," *Science,* 153: 1199–1205 (September 9, 1966).

19 Irene B. Taeuber, *The Population of Japan,* Princeton: Princeton University Press, 1958.

20 See J. Mayone Stycos, *Family and Fertility in Puerto Rico,* New York: Columbia University Press, 1955, and Stycos' numerous studies of factors affecting fertility in a

number of Latin American countries, which have been collected under the title *Human Fertility in Latin America,* Ithaca, N.Y.: Cornell University Press, 1968.

21 Kingsley Davis, "Institutional Patterns Favoring High Fertility in Underdeveloped Areas," *Eugenics Quarterly,* 2: 33–39 (March 1955).

22 The role governments may play in encouraging fertility regulation in underdeveloped areas is stressed by Ryder in a valuable discussion of the contrasts between the situations of Europe in the past and of Asia today with respect to fertility. Norman B. Ryder, "Fertility," in Philip M. Hauser and Otis Dudley Duncan (eds.), *The Study of Population: An Inventory and Appraisal,* Chicago: University of Chicago Press, 1959, pp. 429–434.

23 Taeuber, *op. cit.,* pp. 29–34.

24 Kingsley Davis, *The Population of India and Pakistan,* Princeton: Princeton University Press, 1951, p. 216.

25 Rushton Coulborn, "A Comparative Study of Feudalism," in Coulborn (ed.), *Feudalism in History,* Princeton: Princeton University Press, 1956, p. 185.

26 Edwin O. Reischauer, "Japanese Feudalism," in *ibid.,* p. 48.

27 O. E. Baker, "Population Trends in Relation to Land Utilization," in *Proceedings of the Second International Conference of Agricultural Economists,* Menasha, Wisconsin, 1933, p. 284.

28 Irene B. Taeuber, "The Future of Transitional Areas," in Paul K. Hatt (ed.), *World Population and Future Resources,* New York: American Book Company, 1952, p. 28.

CHAPTER 5

1 Pascal K. Whelpton and Clyde V. Kiser (eds.), *Social and Psychological Factors Affecting Fertility,* 5 vols., New York: Milbank Memorial Fund, 1946, 1950, 1952, 1954, and 1958, Vol. I, Part I.

2 Kurt B. Mayer, *The Population of Switzerland,* New York: Columbia University Press, 1952, pp. 110–111; William Petersen, *Planned Migration: The Social Determinants of the Dutch-Canadian Movement,* Berkeley and Los Angeles: University of California Press, 1955, pp. 35–41; see also the remarks by Ronald Freedman, "Comment," in National Bureau of Economic Research, *Demographic and*

Economic Change in Developed Countries, Princeton: Princeton University Press, 1960, p. 76.

3 Ronald Freedman, Pascal K. Whelpton, and Arthur A. Campbell, *Family Planning, Sterility and Population Growth,* New York: McGraw-Hill Book Co., 1959, pp. 273–288; Pascal K. Whelpton, Arthur A. Campbell, and John E. Patterson, *Fertility and Family Planning in the United States,* Princeton: Princeton University Press, 1966, pp. 70–92; Charles F. Westoff, Robert G. Potter, Jr., Philip C. Sagi, and Eliot G. Mishler, *Family Growth in Metropolitan America,* Princeton: Princeton University Press, 1961, p. 191; Charles F. Westoff, Robert G. Potter, Jr., and Philip C. Sagi, *The Third Child,* Princeton: Princeton University Press, 1963, pp. 231–245.

4 Will Herberg, *Protestant-Catholic-Jew,* New York: Doubleday Anchor Books, 1960, Chap. 10; Nathan Glazer, *American Judaism,* Chicago: University of Chicago Press, 1957; Gerhard Lenski, *The Religious Factor,* New York: Doubleday Anchor Books, 1963.

5 The studies cited in note 3 are chiefly concerned with religious differences in fertility *desires* and *expectations.*

6 Clyde V. Kiser, *Group Differences in Urban Fertility,* Baltimore: Williams and Wilkins Co., 1942, pp. 38–40; and "Differential Fertility in the United States," in National Bureau of Economic Research, *op. cit.,* pp. 87–89.

7 A. J. Jaffe, "Urbanization and Fertility," *American Journal of Sociology,* 48: 48–60 (July 1942).

8 This section in particular, but also much of the rest of the chapter, draws heavily on Dennis H. Wrong, *Class Fertility Trends in Western Nations,* unpublished Ph.D. dissertation, Columbia University, 1956. The findings and conclusions of this study are summarized in Wrong, "Trends in Class Fertility in Western Nations," *Canadian Journal of Economics and Political Science,* 24: 216–229 (May 1958). A briefer comparative survey of class fertility differences in Europe which reaches much the same general conclusions is Gwendolyn Z. Johnson, "Differential Fertility in European Countries," in National Bureau of Economic Research, *op. cit.,* pp. 36–76.

9 Krause has recently challenged this assumption, arguing that a positive correlation between class and fertility may have existed in western Europe before the industrial revolution. The present writer's survey of some of the evidence,

however, suggests precisely the opposite conclusion. See J. T. Krause, "Some Neglected Factors in the English Industrial Revolution," *Journal of Economic History*, 19: 531–534 (Dec. 1959). Compare Dennis H. Wrong, "Class Fertility Differentials Before 1850," *Social Research*, 25: 70–86 (Spring 1958).

10 Charles F. Westoff, "'Differential Fertility in the United States: 1900 to 1950," *American Sociological Review*, 19: 549–561 (Oct. 1954); Wilson H. Grabill, Clyde V. Kiser, and Pascal K. Whelpton, *The Fertility of American Women*, New York: John Wiley and Sons, 1958, pp. 173–184; Johnson, *op. cit.*, pp. 60–70; Dennis H. Wrong, "Class Fertility Differentials in England and Wales," *The Milbank Memorial Fund Quarterly*, 38: 37–47 (Jan. 1960).

11 Clyde V. Kiser, "Fertility Trends and Differentials in the United States," in Joseph J. Spengler and Otis Dudley Duncan (eds.), *Demographic Analysis: Selected Readings*, Glencoe, Ill.: The Free Press, 1956, pp. 177–179.

12 Wrong, *Class Fertility Trends in Western Nations, op. cit.*, Chap. 6.

13 Karl A. Edin and Edward P. Hutchinson, *Studies of Differential Fertility in Sweden*, London: P. S. King and Sons, 1935.

14 Whelpton and Kiser, *op. cit.*, Vol. I, Part II.

15 E. Lewis-Faning, *Family Limitation and Its Influence on Human Fertility During the Past Fifty Years* (Papers of the Royal Commission on Population, Vol. I), London: His Majesty's Stationery Office, 1948, p. 10.

16 Whelpton and Kiser, *op. cit.*, Vol. II, Part IX.

17 Charles F. Westoff, "The Changing Focus of Differential Fertility Research: The Social Mobility Hypothesis," *The Milbank Memorial Fund Quarterly*, 31: 24–38 (Jan. 1953); E. Digby Baltzell, "Social Mobility and Fertility Within an Elite Group," *The Milbank Memorial Fund Quarterly*, 31: 412–420 (Oct. 1953).

18 Whelpton, Campbell and Patterson, *op. cit.*, pp. 123–124.

19 Whelpton and Kiser, *op. cit.*

20 Clyde V. Kiser and Pascal K. Whelpton, "Résumé of the Indianapolis Study of Social and Psychological Factors Affecting Fertility," *Population Studies*, 7: 107–109 (Nov. 1953).

21 See the studies cited in Note 3 and David Goldberg, "Some Recent Developments in American Fertility Research," in National Bureau of Economic Research, *op. cit.*, pp. 137–151.

22 Freedman, Whelpton, and Campbell, *op. cit.*, p. 405.

23 J. Mayone Stycos, *Family and Fertility in Puerto Rico,* New York: Columbia University Press, 1955; Reuben Hill, J. Mayone Stycos, and Kurt W. Back, *The Family and Population Control: A Puerto Rico Experiment in Social Change,* Chapel Hill: University of North Carolina Press, 1959; Lee Rainwater, assisted by Karol Kane Weinstein, *And the Poor Get Children,* Chicago: Quadrangle Books, 1960; Judith Blake, *Family Structure in Jamaica,* Glencoe, Ill.: The Free Press, 1961; J. Mayone Stycos and Kurt W. Back, *The Control of Human Fertility in Jamaica,* Ithaca, N.Y.: Cornell University Press, 1964.

24 Robert Gutman, review of *And the Poor Get Children* in *American Sociological Review,* 26: 105 (Feb. 1961).

25 Philip M. Hauser and Otis Dudley Duncan (eds.), *The Study of Population: An Inventory and Appraisal,* Chicago: University of Chicago Press, 1959, pp. 100–102.

26 See Dennis H. Wrong, review of *The Study of Population: An Inventory and Appraisal,* in *Social Forces,* 37: 74 (Oct. 1959).

27 George J. Stolnitz, "Population Composition and Fertility Trends," *American Sociological Review,* 21: 743 (Dec. 1956); Hauser and Duncan, *op. cit.*, pp. 96–100.

28 Norman B. Ryder, "Fertility," in *ibid.*, pp. 428–434.

29 Wrong, "Trends in Class Fertility in Western Nations," *op. cit.*, pp. 227–229.

CHAPTER 6

1 Donald R. Taft and Richard Robbins, *International Migrations,* New York: The Ronald Press, 1955, p. 3.

2 *Ibid.*, pp. 5–6.

3 William Petersen, "A General Typology of Migration," *American Sociological Review,* 23: 258 (June 1958).

4 Oscar Handlin and others, *The Positive Contribution by Immigrants,* Paris: Unesco, 1955.

5 Petersen, *op. cit.*, pp. 256–266. The remainder of this section relies heavily on Petersen's discussion.

6 *Ibid.*, p. 258.

7 *Ibid.*, p. 261.

8 *Ibid.*, p. 263.

9 Kingsley Davis, *Human Society*, New York: Macmillan Company, 1949, pp. 590–592.

10 William Petersen, *Some Factors Influencing Postwar Emigration from the Netherlands* (Publications of the Research Group for European Migration Problems VI), The Hague: Martinus Nijhoff, 1952, p. 42.

11 Taft and Robbins, *op. cit.*, p. 30.

12 Petersen, "A General Typology of Migration," *op. cit.*, pp. 258–259.

13 *Ibid.*, p. 263.

14 Dudley Kirk, "European Migrations: Prewar Trends and Future Prospects," in Milbank Memorial Fund, *Postwar Problems of Migration,* New York: Milbank Memorial Fund, 1948, p. 58.

15 For a variety of discussions of this problem, summarizing it and arriving in some cases at differing conclusions, see Harry Jerome, *Migration and Business Cycles,* New York: National Bureau of Economic Research, 1926; Brinley Thomas, "The Economic Aspect," in Oscar Handlin and others, *op. cit.,* pp. 165–185; David C. Corbett, *Canada's Immigration Policy,* Toronto: University of Toronto Press, 1957, Chaps. 4 and 5; William Petersen, *Planned Migration: The Social Determinants of the Dutch-Canadian Movement,* Berkeley and Los Angeles: University of California Press, 1955, pp. 210–221; Joseph J. Spengler, "The Economic Effects of Migration," in Milbank Memorial Fund, *Selected Studies of Migration Since World War II,* New York: Milbank Memorial Fund, 1958, pp. 189–192.

16 Petersen, "A General Typology of Migration," *op. cit.,* p. 258.

17 For a brilliant discussion of these two concepts or ideologies in their bearing on actual American experience, see Nathan Glazer, "Ethnic Groups in America: From National Culture to Ideology," in Morroe Berger, Theodore Abel, and Charles H. Page (eds.), *Freedom and Control in Modern Society,* New York: D. Van Nostrand, 1954, pp. 158–173.

See also Marcus Lee Hansen, *The Immigrant in American History*, Cambridge: Harvard University Press, 1940; and Oscar Handlin, *The Uprooted*, Boston: Little, Brown and Company, 1951.

18 Kirk, *op. cit.*, pp. 57–60.

19 Dudley Kirk, "Major Migrations Since World War II," in Milbank Memorial Fund, *Selected Studies of Migration Since World War II*, pp. 17–19.

20 Petersen, *Planned Migration: The Social Determinants of the Dutch-Canadian Movement, op. cit.*, Part I.

21 Hannah Arendt, *The Origins of Totalitarianism*, New York: Harcourt, Brace & Co., 1951, p. 396.

22 Irene B. Taeuber, "Migration and the Population Potential of Monsoon Asia," in Milbank Memorial Fund, *Postwar Problems of Migration*, p. 28.

23 Petersen, *Planned Migration, op. cit.*, pp. 194–196, 202–210.

24 Warren S. Thompson, *Population Problems*, 3rd ed., New York: McGraw-Hill Book Co., 1942, p. 382.

CHAPTER 7

1 James A. Field, *Essays on Population and Other Papers*, Chicago: University of Chicago Press, 1931, p. 250.

2 T. R. Malthus, *An Essay on Population*, 2 vols., London: J. M. Dent and Sons, New York: E. P. Dutton and Co. (Everyman's Library, No. 692), 1914, Vol. I, pp. 18–19.

3 *Ibid.*, p. 14.

4 *Ibid.*, p. 13.

5 See especially his argument in *ibid.*, Vol. II, pp. 157–159.

6 Kingsley Davis, *Human Society*, New York: Macmillan Company, 1949, p. 612.

7 Ian Bowen, *Population*, London: James Nisbet and Co., Cambridge: Cambridge University Press (Cambridge Economic Handbooks), 1954, p. 105.

8 Malthus, *op. cit.*, Vol. II, p. 140. See the analysis of Malthus' ambiguities on the subject of the standard of living and fertility by D. E. C. Eversley, *Social Theories of Fertility and the Malthusian Debate*, Oxford: The Clarendon Press, 1959, pp. 249–257.

9 Eversley, *ibid.*, p. 279.

10 For the Catholic position, see William J. Gibbons, "The Catholic Value System in Relation to Human Fertility," in George F. Mair (ed.), *Studies in Population,* Princeton: Princeton University Press, 1949, pp. 108–134; for a general account of Christian and Jewish attitudes towards the family and fertility, see Richard Fagley, *The Population Explosion and Christian Responsibility,* New York: Oxford University Press, 1960; for the Communist position, see Frank Lorimer, "Population Policy and Politics in the Communist World," in Philip M. Hauser (ed.), *Population and World Politics,* Glencoe, Ill.: The Free Press, 1958, pp. 214–236.

11 For two extreme statements of the neo-Malthusian viewpoint, see William Vogt, *Road to Survival,* New York: William Sloane Associates, 1948; and Robert C. Cook, *Human Fertility: the Modern Dilemma,* New York: William Sloane Associates, 1951.

12 Two doctrinaire statements of the neo-Godwinian position are Josué de Castro, *The Geography of Hunger,* Boston: Little, Brown and Co., 1952; and Jacob Oser, *Must Men Starve?* New York: Abelard-Schuman, 1957.

13 Actually, interplanetary migration as a solution to overpopulation is both economically and sociologically impossible. See Lincoln and Alice Day, *Too Many Americans,* Boston: Houghton Mifflin Co., 1964, pp. 168–170.

14 One of the few broad, nontechnical books on the subject which carefully distinguishes between what is *possible* and what is *probable* is Harrison Brown's valuable *The Challenge of Man's Future,* New York: The Viking Press, 1954, Chap. 7.

15 Their point of view is well represented by Joseph J. Spengler, "The Population Obstacle to Economic Betterment," in Joseph J. Spengler and Otis Dudley Duncan (eds.), *Population Theory and Policy: Selected Readings,* Glencoe, Ill.: The Free Press, 1956, pp. 305–316; and Kingsley Davis, "Population and the Further Spread of Industrial Society," in *ibid.,* pp. 317–333. See also United Nations, *The Determinants and Consequences of Population Trends,* New York: United Nations, 1953, pp. 282–284.

16 See, for example, Vogt, *op. cit.;* and Fairfield Osborn, *Our Plundered Planet,* Boston: Little, Brown and Co., 1950, Chap. 5.

17 Joseph J. Spengler, "The Aesthetics of Population," *Population Bulletin,* 13: 61–75 (June 1957).

18 See Simon Kuznets, "Regional Economic Trends and Levels of Living," in Hauser, *op. cit.*, pp. 79–117; and Everett Hagen, "World Economic Trends and Living Standards," in *ibid.*, pp. 118–136; United Nations, *op. cit.*, Chap. 15.

19 Kuznets, *op. cit.*, pp. 87–91.

20 Kingsley Davis, *The Population of India and Pakistan*, Princeton: Princeton University Press, 1951, Chap. 21.

21 Ansley J. Coale and Edgar M. Hoover have shown that at present rates of economic growth, per capita income in India would increase by nearly 40 per cent if the birth rate fell by half in one generation. See Coale and Hoover, *Population Growth and Economic Development in Low-Income Countries,* Princeton: Princeton University Press, 1958, p. 272.

22 Puerto Rico has already experienced a sharp decline in fertility which may be a harbinger of the future of other Latin-American countries. See Christopher Tietze, "Human Fertility in Latin America," The American Academy of Political and Social Science, *The Annals,* 316: 84–93 (March 1958).

23 Irene B. Taeuber, "Population Policies in Communist China," *Population Index,* 22: 261–273 (Oct. 1956).

24 See J. Mayone Stycos, "A Critique of the Traditional Planned Parenthood Approach in Underdeveloped Areas," in Clyde V. Kiser (ed.), *Research in Family Planning,* Princeton: Princeton University Press, 1962, pp. 477–501.

25 This is one of the major themes of Warren S. Thompson's *Population and Progress in the Far East,* Chicago: University of Chicago Press, 1959.

26 G. L. Arnold, *The Pattern of World Conflict,* New York: The Dial Press, 1955, pp. 202–227; see also Morris Watnick, "The Appeal of Communism to the Peoples of Underdeveloped Areas," in Reinhard Bendix and Seymour Martin Lipset (eds.), *Class, Status and Power: A Reader in Social Stratification,* Glencoe, Ill.: The Free Press, 1966, 2nd ed., pp. 428–436.

Selected Readings

General

UNITED NATIONS, *Determinants and Consequences of Population Trends,* New York: United Nations, Department of Social Affairs, Population Division, 1953.

An exhaustive and lucid summary of virtually all available theories and facts about population and their bearing on social and economic trends. Includes the most complete bibliography extant.

SPENGLER, JOSEPH J. and OTIS DUDLEY DUNCAN (eds.), *Demographic Analysis: Selected Readings,* Glencoe, Ill.: The Free Press, 1956.

A collection of readings dealing with empirical, rather than methodological or theoretical, studies of population.

HAUSER, PHILIP M. and OTIS DUDLEY DUNCAN (eds.), *The Study of Population: An Inventory and Appraisal,* Chicago: University of Chicago Press, 1959.

As the title implies, this monumental symposium deals with the discipline of population study rather than with its object. Few disciplines have ever been so comprehensively surveyed by their leading practitioners. Some of the contributions are fairly technical.

DAVIS, KINGSLEY, *Human Society,* New York: Macmillan Company, 1949, Chapters 20–21.

The chapters on population in this well-known sociology text provide a sociologically sophisticated introduction to the subject.

PETERSEN, WILLIAM, *Population,* New York: Macmillan Company, 1961.

The best introductory text on population yet to appear. Greatly exceeds its predecessors in sociological insight and theoretical sophistication.

THOMLINSON, RALPH, *Population Dynamics*, New York: Random House, 1965.

A highly readable and comprehensive introductory textbook. Like Petersen, it is written for the sociologist as much as for the formal demographer.

FREEDMAN, RONALD (ed.), *Population: The Vital Revolution*, New York: Doubleday Anchor Books, 1964.

A collection of articles by most of America's leading students of population on all aspects of American and world population.

World Population Growth and Distribution

CARR-SAUNDERS, A. M., *World Population*, Oxford: The Clarendon Press, 1936.

Outdated but still perhaps the best general exposition of past world population growth and distribution available. Unequaled for comprehensiveness and readability.

WOYTINSKY, W. S. and E. S. WOYTINSKY, *World Population and Production: Trends and Outlook*, New York: The Twentieth Century Fund, 1953.

An encyclopaedic volume on demographic, social, and economic data and trends. An invaluable sourcebook for historical statistical information.

HAUSER, PHILIP M. (ed.), *Population and World Politics*, Glencoe, Ill.: The Free Press, 1958.

The scope of this collection is rather wider than the title implies, including demographic and economic analyses by leading authorities. The contributors are a blue-ribbon group consisting of nearly all the best-known and most productive American populationists as well as several equally well-known economists.

PETERSEN, WILLIAM, *The Politics of Population*, New York, N.Y.: Doubleday and Co., 1964.

A wide-ranging collection of essays on population theory, the population of Europe, internal and international migration and other subjects.

Regional Case Studies

DAVIS, KINGSLEY, *The Population of India and Pakistan,* Princeton: Princeton University Press, 1951.

MAYER, KURT B., *The Population of Switzerland,* New York: Columbia University Press, 1952.

ROYAL COMMISSION ON POPULATION, *Report,* London: His Majesty's Stationery Office, 1949.

TAEUBER, IRENE B., *The Population of Japan,* Princeton: Princeton University Press, 1958.

All of these are clearly written accounts of the demography and the socioeconomic structure of a number of contemporary nations. The British *Report* is somewhat technical in places. For analyses of American population, see especially the following titles listed above: Petersen, *Population,* Chapters 2–11; Freedman, *Population: The Vital Revolution,* Chapters 6–10.

Mortality

DUBLIN, LOUIS I., ALFRED J. LOTKA and MORTIMER SPIEGELMAN, *Length of Life,* New York: Ronald Press, 1949.

An exhaustive review of mortality trends and patterns in the United States with particular emphasis on the uses of the life table. Frequently rather technical.

MILBANK MEMORIAL FUND, *Trends and Differentials in Mortality,* New York: Milbank Memorial Fund, 1956.

A collection of papers broadly covering recent world-wide developments in mortality and their implications for the future.

Fertility, Differential Fertility, and Family Planning

DAVIS, KINGSLEY and JUDITH BLAKE, "Social Structure and Fertility: An Analytic Framework," *Economic Development and Cultural Change,* 4: 211–235 (April 1956).

Although this bibliography is intended to include only books, an exception has been made in the case of this valuable article, which provides an over-all conceptual ordering for the study of fertility and the factors affecting it.

EVERSLEY, D. E. C., *Social Theories of Fertility and the Malthusian Debate,* Oxford: The Clarendon Press, 1959.

A work of intellectual history that manages to achieve genuine relevance to contemporary fertility theory.

WHELPTON, PASCAL K., ARTHUR A. CAMPBELL, and JOHN E. PATTERSON, *Fertility and Family Planning in the United States,* Princeton: Princeton University Press, 1966.

The widest, most comprehensive and methodologically careful study yet to be made employing opinion survey methods to explore the attitudes of contemporary Americans towards family size, contraceptive usage, and desired size of family. Utilizes the data to estimate the incidence of sterility and probable future trends in fertility. Contains a wealth of suggestive information, and summarizes earlier studies by the same authors and others.

GRABILL, WILSON H., CLYDE V. KISER and PASCAL K. WHELPTON, *The Fertility of American Women,* New York: John Wiley and Sons, 1958.

A volume in the Census Monograph Series which exhaustively and ingeniously summarizes American census data, past and present, on current fertility measures, differential fertility, and cohort fertility.

LORIMER, FRANK and Others, *Culture and Human Fertility,* Paris: United Nations Educational, Scientific and Cultural Organization, 1954.

A somewhat disorderly volume crammed with suggestive data and interpretation. Includes several papers by anthropologists on fertility and its determinants in primitive societies.

KISER, CLYDE V. (ed.), *Research in Family Planning,* Princeton: Princeton University Press, 1962.

A huge symposium on methods of fertility control, family planning, and research problems in the study of family planning viewed in world-wide perspective.

RAINWATER, LEE with the assistance of KAROL KANE WEINSTEIN, *And the Poor Get Children,* Chicago: Quadrangle Books, 1960.

STYCOS, J. MAYONE, *Family and Fertility in Puerto Rico,* New York: Columbia University Press, 1955.

Both these books go further than previous studies in relating fertility, family planning, and contraceptive usage to sexuality and character structure as these are shaped by culture. The Rainwater book deals with a sample of American working-class men and women, while the Stycos book deals with low-income Puerto Rican families.

Migration

TAFT, DONALD and RICHARD ROBBINS, *International Migrations,* New York: The Ronald Press, 1955.

A competent and inclusive textbook.

MILBANK MEMORIAL FUND, *Selected Studies of Migration Since World War II,* New York: Milbank Memorial Fund, 1958.

A valuable symposium on all of the demographic aspects of the subject.

PETERSEN, WILLIAM, *Planned Migration: The Social Determinants of the Dutch-Canadian Movement,* Berkeley and Los Angeles: University of California Press, 1955.

A detailed study of a particular migratory movement with reference to both the country of origin and the country of destination. Far more than a case study in its theoretical suggestiveness and analysis of the ideological and political determinants of governmental immigration and emigration policies.

World Resources, Economic Growth, and the Malthusian Problem

MALTHUS, THOMAS, JULIAN HUXLEY and FREDERICK OSBORN, *On Population,* New York: The New American Library, 1960.

This low-price paperback includes Malthus' "A Summary View of the Principle of Population," his final statement of his theory, as well as two excellent essays on the problems created by the present world population explosion by Huxley and Osborn.

BROWN, HARRISON, *The Challenge of Man's Future,* New York: The Viking Press (Compass Books), 1954.

   A somewhat depressing but well-written and sophisticated review of world population and resources problems. Far superior to the general run of non-technical books on this subject.

FRANCIS, ROY G. (ed.), *The Population Ahead,* Minneapolis: University of Minnesota Press, 1958.

HAUSER, PHILIP M. (ed.), *The Population Dilemma,* Englewood Cliffs, N.J.: Prentice-Hall, Inc., 1963.

   Two collections of papers and discussions by leading population students, economists, and resource specialists.

Demographic Techniques

BARCLAY, GEORGE W., *Techniques of Population Analysis,* New York: John Wiley and Sons, 1958.

   Probably the best introductory manual on methodology.

Index

Abortion: influence on fertility, 44–46; in Japan and West, 57, 65; Christian opposition, 64; as form of birth control, 116

Abstinence, sexual, 46, 57, 102

Accidents, as cause of death, 38–39

Africa: pre-agricultural parts, 11; population, 13; growth rate, 12, 24; growth since 1650, 14; births-deaths balance, 15–17, 19; origin of man in, 86; density, 94, 115; birth control, 112

Age: as population characteristic, 2, 6, 8; at marriage, 21, 59, 60, 64, 102, 105; in relation to death rates, 27–37; and fecundity, 43; at childbearing, 59, 60; and migration, 98

Anti-Malthusianism, 108, 113, 116

Arendt, Hannah, 23, 122, 130

Arnold, G. L., 117, 132

Asia: population, 12–14; births-deaths balance, 16; density, 21, 115; future growth, 24; joint family system, 63, 65–66; future fertility decline, 64, 66; migration as solution for, 94–95; restricted immigration of Asians, 94, 99; birth control, 112; peasant agriculture, 114; need for population policy, 116

Australasia: population, 13 (see under Oceania); births-deaths balance, 19; death rates, 26

Australia: birth rate, 16; births-deaths balance, 16; population, 18; death rate, 30–31; life expectancy, 34; post-war fertility rise, 61; migration to, 88, 93; density, 109

Baby boom, 48, 58–62, 78

Baker, O. E., 66, 122

Belgium, 69

Birth control: and decline of fertility, 56–58; methods, 57; Catholic opposition to, 62; motivation for use, 63–64; diffusion of, 76–77; Malthus on, 102, 105; religion and ideology, 107–108; advocates, 110; and economic development, 111–113; appeal of methods, 116; see also Contraception, Family planning

Birth rates, see Fertility

Births, 1–4, 6; registration,

139